Attracting
Terrific
People

Attracting Terrific People

How to find—and keep— the people who bring your life joy

LILLIAN GLASS, PH.D.

ST. MARTIN'S GRIFFIN
NEW YORK

DESIGN BY BARBARA M. BACHMAN

Library of Congress Cataloging-in-Publication Data

Glass, Lillian
    Attracting terrific people: how to find, and keep, the people who bring your life joy / Lillian Glass.
        p. cm.
    Includes index.
    ISBN 0-312-18045-4
    1. Interpersonal relations. 2. Interpersonal attraction.
    I. Title.
    HM132.G544 1997
    646.7—dc21   96-44911
                                                                        CIP

First St. Martin's Griffin Edition: March 1998

10 9 8 7 6 5 4 3 2 1

To Abraham ''Anthony'' Glass—

I dedicate this book to you. You were truly a Terrific Person in every sense of the word. I am who I am today only because of your love, dedication, encouragement, and farsightedness. You let me reach for the stars and beyond and I shall continue to honor your wishes and "fulfill my dreams."

Daddy, I will always love you and you will always be with me!

—Lillian Glass
Oct. 2, 1996

Acknowledgments

I wish to thank literary agent Toni Lopopolo who enabled me to get my message of "global peace through communication" out in book form.

To my terrific, sharp, and creative editor, Heather Jackson, whose enthusiasm for this project motivated me to go that extra mile. She has all of the ingredients necessary to end up at the very top of her field, as she is truly a credit to her profession.

I also wish to thank the sales staff, marketing department, and the publicity department at St. Martin's Press for believing in this project and doing whatever it took to make this project the success that it is.

I wish to thank my mother—my most terrific friend in the world—Rosalie Glass, for her insight and words of wisdom and teachings that permeate this book. To my terrific brother Manny for his wisdom, understanding, and terrific sense of humor.

To my most favorite terrific being in the entire world—Lambear—my sidekick. Even though he is a canine terrific person, he made writing this book an even more pleasant experience than it already was. I thank him for his cuddle breaks, "come play with me" breaks, and for making me laugh by hopping up onto my desk, sprawling across the manuscript, and refusing to get up until he was loved up with affection—demonstrating what is really important in life.

And to some of my other favorite terrific people, whom I respect and admire, who have graced my life in ways that they may not even realize. I cherish them from the bottom of my heart, especially Al, Alan, Annie, Armand, Arnold, Ashley, Ben, Beth, Bikram, Bill, Bob, Brian, Carol, Charles, Christina, Christopher, Dana, Darryl, Dean, Dee, Dena, Diane, Dolly, Don, Ed, Edie, Elizabeth, Eric, Fran, Frank, Harlan, Harvey, Henry, Howard, Jaroslav, Isaac, Irene, Jeffrey, Jim, Julio, Irene, June, Kirk, Larry, Lily, Lisa, Lucille, Marty, Maura, Merna, Mickey, Michael, Nancy, Nat, Nina, Norman, Pam, Paul, Peter, Rene, Richard, Rita, Robert, Rosalie, Sabina, Sean, Simon, Steve, Stuart, Susan, Suzanne, Tracie, Tony, and Wanda.

I thank them for being an inspiration for many of the scenarios discussed in this book. I am a better person because they are in my life.

Contents

Introduction

*I*f you were granted just one wish, besides good health, that would bring you a fulfilling and truly happy life, what would that wish be?

Would you wish to:

(a) *be incredibly wealthy*

(b) *be world famous*

(c) *have incredible sex appeal*

(d) *be the best in your chosen field*

(e) *be the most physically attractive person*

(f) *have great intelligence or*

(g) *have only "terrific" people in your life?*

If you chose "g," you are highly astute. Choosing terrific people to grace your life is the only choice that can bring about total life fulfillment. You need other people to appreciate your special qualities, or this list has no relevance.

It doesn't matter whether you are the world's greatest singer, dancer, athlete, doctor, lawyer, lover, sex symbol, or comedian. If you don't have others in your life who recognize your talents and appreciate your specialness then life has very little meaning.

Tom is a world-renowned speaker. He travels three hundred days a year for speaking engagements around the globe. Recently, after finishing a speech and looking out at the twenty-five thousand people giving him a standing ovation, he got choked up. The crowd loved him and wouldn't stop clapping. People rushed to the stage to talk to him, to touch him, to shake his hand, to tell him how much his talk affected them. Brilliant and powerful men in designer suits handed him their cards and invited him to lunch. Beautiful women surrounded him; some smiling, some cooing flirtatiously, others with tears in their eyes, telling him how much his talk moved them.

Tom felt like a rock star. He felt higher than any drug or any drink could take him. Both his head and his heart were pounding so hard, he thought he was going to explode from all the excitement. After an hour of this heady experience, he retreated to his hotel room—alone. He was so excited that he wanted to immediately get on the phone and share his experience with someone. Instinctively, he picked up the receiver—then realized he had nobody to call. Constantly being on the road had cost him his marriage and his personal life. He had lost contact with so many people he had been close to at one time. The silence was deafening.

Although Tom was being praised and adulated by thousands, he had no special people in his life to share in this peak experience. It was this grim realization that led him to rethink what was important to him. As a result, he cut back drastically on his lecture schedule, and now has many great friends in his life whom he cherishes and whom he doesn't take for granted. They have given a new meaning to the quality of his life.

We not only need people to acknowledge us and to share our intimate feelings with, but we need people to make our lives successful. The great Walt Disney was well aware of this truth. Throughout his many successes, he never forgot who was truly responsible for seeing his dream become a reality. As he said, ''Whatever we have accomplished has been because other people have helped us.''

No matter how many awards and honors Disney received, he always gave credit to others where credit was due.

You cannot clap with just one hand. You need two hands to make a sound. Similarly, you cannot make things happen in your life by yourself. You need other people to help you.

No matter what all the self-help books say—"you can do it on your own," "you can make it if you try," "you can visualize your success," "develop more self-confidence," "increase your inner strength by increasing your outer strength," "you can get to the top only if you believe in yourself and not give in to your demons,"—the truth is that *you cannot do it on your own*. You will still fail to achieve the success you desire if you ignore the most essential element necessary for reaching your goal: attracting other people who can help and assist you. In essence, you cannot make anything happen without the help of other people in your life.

Look at the beauty and the success of Alcoholics Anonymous, and other related twelve-step programs. People are helped by other people. People are there to hold the hands of others, to help them walk until they run, and to be there to catch them in case they fall. They are there to lend their moral support, their experience, and their guidance.

Many people lent their support and guidance to some of the most famous people of our generation: television hostess Oprah Winfrey, President Bill Clinton, media mogul Ted Turner, Academy Award–winner Tom Hanks, and actress Sharon Stone. As brilliant and talented as they are, if it weren't for other people in their lives who supported them enough to give them the chance to live out their dreams, they would not be famous today. Certainly it was their own hard work and diligence that helped them to succeed, but they were able to reach the top only because other people spoke the kind words that encouraged them or did just the right small favor at just the right moment. If you take a really good look at the lives of successful people, you will quickly realize that they have all had terrific people in their corner every step of the way, offering belief and support.

Even though it may be wonderful to be wealthy, brilliant, rich, and famous, if you have nobody to give you a kind or an encouraging word, or with whom to share things, all the wealth, intelligence, and fame in the world mean little or nothing at all.

No matter what you do, you need other people to make life worthwhile. If you want to live a fulfilled life, you need to know how to attract, how to find, and how to keep the people who will bring you joy. Without them life is meaningless.

THIS IS NOT a new concept. Every major religion recognizes the importance of having good and wonderful people in one's life from the Talmud to the Koran, from the New Testament to the Bhagavad Gita, from Buddhist doctrines to the teachings of Lao-tzu.

As early as the fifth century B.C., the great philosopher Confucius, who influenced civilization throughout East Asia, relayed the importance of surrounding oneself with "good" people and the positive effect that doing so has on our lives. Noted psychologist Abraham Maslow discussed "terrific people" and how special and unique they were in his theories of what constituted "self-actualized" people.

In our culture, the concept of having wonderful people in our life has been important for the past six decades, ever since Dale Carnegie's famous book, *How to Win Friends and Influence People,* was published in 1936. A mainstay in people's lives around the world, this classic has continued to sell millions of copies worldwide because it has transformed the lives of untold numbers of people.

But even though it was a wonderful book for its time, and although several of Dale Carnegie's principles still apply, many do not work in today.

For example, concepts such as these are no longer effective: *"constantly using a person's name in a conversation because it is the sweetest and most important sound in any language; never telling a man he is wrong; getting the other person to say 'yes, yes' immediately; letting the other man do a great deal of the talking; letting the other fellow feel that the idea is his; beginning with praise and appreciation; calling attention to people's mistakes indirectly; talking about your own mistakes before criticizing the other person; and praising the slightest improvement; being hearty in your approbation and lavish your praise."* People in today's society are too hip, too aware, too sophisticated, and can see right through many of these manipulative tactics, which many deem as phony and insincere.

Since the world today is so vastly different from the one in which Dale Carnegie lived, with computers, telecommunication systems, satellite systems, and a vastly different psychological world of new values, attitudes, moral standards, and beliefs, we need new tools to help us today.

Hence, the main reason for this book. As a communications consultant who has worked with Hollywood's A-list of top stars, political figures, sports heroes, singers, supermodels, movie stars, talk-show hosts, news anchors, CEOs of top companies, best-selling authors, and even international leaders who have achieved great things in their lives, I learned a great deal from them. I learned the secret of success. The common thread that made all of these individuals' successes was that these *"terrific" people knew how to attract other "terrific" people to their team who, in turn, helped them to the top.*

Another inspiration for writing *Attracting Terrific People* took shape while I was lecturing across the country about my book *Toxic People: 10 Ways of Dealing with People Who Make Your Life Miserable* (St. Martin's Press, 1997). Day after day, people from the audience would come up to me with the same questions: "Where are all the 'terrific people'? How can I attract more 'terrific people' to my life?" I soon realized that these questions deserved much more than the brief response that I could give them after a lecture. The antidote to dealing with "toxic people" was learning how to attract and how to keep "terrific" people in one's life in order to buffer the "toxins."

The techniques I share with you in *Attracting Terrific People* have worked not only for my thousands of clients, but also for me personally. They have transformed my life—and, in healing myself, I have been able to heal others.

Like you, I have also felt shy, insecure, and uncomfortable in social situations. Like you, I have felt the searing pain of being rejected and the terrible frustration of not being able to move forward with my life because I was paralyzed by fear and shaky self-esteem. Like you, I have felt lonely, empty, and scared.

But today I no longer feel that way because I have found and am continuing to find terrific people who were happy to work with me rather than against me. I also learned how to become a terrific person myself and give back what the terrific people in my life gave me. As a result, I have never been or continued to be happier and more fulfilled.

By following the techniques in this book, you will learn how to develop richer, deeper, and more meaningful relationships with others. As I have attracted terrific people to my life who have helped me live out my dreams, my confidence level has grown, my career has blossomed, my social life has flourished, and I have learned the joys of passing this happiness on to others.

When you finally realize that you need terrific people in your life, you will have indeed achieved wisdom. This is the secret that can make every aspect of your life work—from finding happiness in love to achieving the ultimate success and financial independence.

What this book is *not* about is finding a "sugar daddy" or rich woman or becoming a gigolo or gold digger, so that you can get people to give you things and support you without your having to work.

Rather, *Attracting Terrific People* is about finding the inner power and drive to do whatever it takes to develop your skills and talents while respecting yourself, maintaining your integrity and dignity, respecting others, and going the extra mile for them—and for yourself.

In the first section of this book, you will learn:

- *why you need and deserve to have terrific people in your life*
- *how having terrific people in your life can help you overcome depression, boredom, and loneliness*
- *how to identify and cherish the terrific people who come your way and who can help you live out your dreams, so that you can have a richer and more meaningful life*
- *where to find terrific people*
- *opening your world to exciting new people who will really change your life for the better*
- *how to attract terrific people*
- *how to discover new ways of communicating with others and presenting yourself in the best way possible*
- *how to overcome your roadblocks of shyness and insecurity*

The second section will focus on:

- *how you can be a terrific person yourself who can give it all back by doing the same for others*
- *how to handle rejection without letting it devastate you*
- *how you can decrease your stress levels so you look and feel better, which will draw more terrific people your way*
- *how you can feel more comfortable taking risks with people*
- *how to develop the security and self-confidence of a winner who is appealing, attractive, and exciting to others.*

The information in this book has helped thousands of my clients change their lives virtually overnight. I have seen countless clients who initially came into my office feeling depressed, lonely, sad, insecure, and hopeless because their lives were filled with dead-end jobs, they never had enough money, they associated with people whom they really didn't like or worse yet, they were constantly around people who made their lives a living hell.

After learning and practicing the techniques in this book, their lives took a one hundred-eighty-degree turn. Suddenly, they had more confidence, they felt more secure, they found out who they were and how they had a right to have a great life filled with great people. They started to dress, stand, sit, and speak with more confidence. They said what they meant and meant what they said. They became more communicative, more open, more verbal in their wants and needs. They no longer tolerated anything or anyone in their lives who didn't contribute to their positive growth. In turn, they became more positive, more giving, and more loving.

Because of their newly found sense of self, they attracted more terrific people around them. They continued on a cycle of being terrific and attracting the terrific, which opened new lives. I saw miracles happen in my office each day. Clients went from feeling shy and insecure to feeling outspoken and self-confident, as though they could do anything they wanted to in life. I watched people go from rags to riches, from being a hermit to being one of the most social individuals in town, from thinking they would never find a mate—and that there was nobody out there for them—to finding the love of their lives.

This book really works! Just take your time reading and rereading it whenever you need to. The stories, which are true accounts of clients and people I know, will inspire you attract, find, keep, and be the most terrific person you ever imagined in your life, thereby opening up a wonderful new and exciting world for you.

　　—Lillian Glass, Ph.D.
　　September, 1996

Chapter 1

Why You Need and Deserve Terrific People in Your Life

- *The World Is Full of Terrific People*
- *Why You Need Terrific People in Your Life*
- *Why Have You Sabotaged Yourself in the Past by Pushing Terrific People Out of Your Life?*
- *People Deserve Terrific People in Their Lives, but for Some It's Overwhelming*
- *Warning Signs of Unworthiness*
- *Steps to Keep Yourself from Sabotaging Your Precious Relationships*
- *Overcoming Your Fears*
- *You Deserve the Best That People Have to Offer*
- *What Knowing Terrific People Can Do for You*

$\mathcal{P}$erhaps the most frequent question I hear, not only from clients and people attending my seminars, but from friends and colleagues alike, is "Where are all the good people?" After countless rounds of disappointment and heartbreak, single women will often ask me, "Are there any decent men out there?" Similarly, men will remark that all the "good women" out there are already taken. I constantly hear statements such as "you can't trust anyone," "people are out to get you," and "it's a dog-eat-dog world."

You can certainly appreciate where these statements are coming from if you turn on the nightly newscasts or watch myriad daytime talk shows. All you seem to see and hear are stories about horribly "toxic" people doing horrible things to each other. Combine what we see and hear in the media with some of our own personal disappointment, rejection, and emotional heartbreak due to "toxic" individuals who have made our lives miserable, and it is not difficult to see why so many people feel so negatively about others.

But the truth of the matter is that statistically these "bad" people we see on the news who perpetrate crimes and these "toxic" individuals we see on our television screens during the day, are not the majority of people. They are on television only because certain "unevolved" programmers think that the bizarre and the hateful and the disturbed create television ratings, which translate into revenue for their stations. What they have failed to realize is that most people don't want to watch these "toxic" people all day long. In fact, research has now shown that people want to be inspired, uplifted, and motivated.

As evidenced in my previous book, *Toxic People,* there are indeed awful people out there who can destroy your self-esteem, your self-worth, and even your life. If you have met and attracted enough of these "toxic people" consistently, it is no wonder that you may feel cynical and unexcited about dealing with other people. You have to realize that you are not alone—that everyone has or had people in their lives who were awful to them. However, those who utilized the techniques I described in *Toxic People* are now happier. Based on the countless letters I receive from readers each day, the techniques have transformed their lives.

One forty-nine-year-old schoolteacher told me she was able to dance and smile for the first time in her life because she cast the burden of her "toxic" control-freak father off her shoulders by "unplugging" him out of her life for good. She reports in her letter that since she shed her father from her life, she's also shed twenty pounds, and has never been happier.

Another businessman used the "humor technique" on his "bossy-bully-boss" while a woman used the "love and kindness technique" on her "bossy-bully sister." In both cases, they noticed immediate results and a more positive effect in terms of how they were treated by the "toxic" person in their lives. The stories are endless, but the results are the same. You *can* deal with the negative people in your life.

Most people are not born bad. In many cases, what happens in their lives and what they choose to do about those circumstances make them turn out good or bad or toxic or terrific.

Juan Carlos's mother was a prostitute, and he had no idea who his father was. He grew up in poverty and squalor. As a little boy, he saw things no person should witness, let alone a child. He saw people getting high on crack cocaine and being totally out of control. He saw graffiti-marked buildings that smelled of urine and vomit. He saw his twelve-year-old neighbor and best friend murdered by a young boy of ten who lived down the block. He saw a baby bleeding from head to toe as she was riddled with bullets in a drive-by shooting. He saw his mother being beaten black-and-blue by one of her "boyfriends." She continued her relationship with him as her son's cries to her fell on deaf ears. Juan Carlos saw the "devil" all of his life and literally lived in hell. One day he was approached by a gang of boys who wanted him to rob a market with them. Fearing their wrath, he told them he had a stomachache and would go another time. The boys didn't buy his story, so they beat him up and told him that they would kill him if he didn't go the next time. Frightened, with tears rolling down his dirty face, Juan Carlos ran for what seemed like miles until he came to a church. There he met the priest, Father John, with whom he shared his dilemma. That night, Father John called upon the boy's mother to ask if Juan Carlos could work at the church cleaning and doing chores in exchange for housing and attending parochial school. Glad to get rid of him, his mother agreed. Juan Carlos took it upon himself to learn whatever he could from Father John. He flourished in his new surroundings, becoming an A student and excelling in sports. He never looked back—only forward. He got a football scholarship to Notre Dame and became an honor student. He went to law school and now is one of the top criminal attorneys in the country. In his spare time, he counsels young gang members in the barrio in East Los Angeles. He has set up a youth center where he coaches all-night basketball games and football games to keep potential gang members off the streets.

Juan Carlos was born under "bad" circumstances, but he wasn't born "bad." He could easily have taken the low road, joined the gang and ended up like most of the young men he grew up with—either in prison or dead. It was because of a terrific person, Father John, that Juan Carlos became who he is today. Juan Carlos has never forgotten it.

THE WORLD IS FULL OF TERRIFIC PEOPLE

Like Father John and Juan Carlos, there are lots of wonderful people with whom you come in contact daily. (These are the people we really need to see on television every day. We are sick and tired of watching the dysfunctional few.) The majority of people are good, want to be good, and want to do good for themselves, for their families, and for others.

There are millions of terrific people in the world. If you haven't found enough of them, you haven't looked hard enough at other people and at yourself.

Terrific people have shown their faces and their true colors during the floods in the Midwest, the hurricanes in Miami, the Malibu fires, the earthquakes in northern and southern California, during the bombings of the World Trade Center in New York and the Federal Building in Oklahoma City. These terrific people came to the rescue. They did whatever they had to do unselfishly in order to help another person—whether it be to comfort a crying child, to pull someone out of rubble and debris, to feed the hungry, clothe the cold, and even breathe life into helpless bodies. Terrific strangers helping other terrific strangers. That is what life is all about and that is what we need to focus on more!

We need to recognize terrific people like the wonderful veterinarian in Los Angeles who gives homeless people's pets free veterinary care. We need a daily dose of stories about people like the anonymous man who went to a children's hospital each day and gave gifts to young cancer patients, with a note stating that this gift was from their ''very special angel'' who was watching over, taking care of, and loving them. He gave generously each day so that a dying child could smile and have something to look forward to.

What about the person who makes it a point to make others' days pleasant in the busiest, most stressful, harried city in the world—New York City—by just smiling at everyone he passes and saying hello to as many people as he can. By acknowledging passersby, he feels that in his own small way, he is making a contribution to their having a happier day.

So, for those who ask, ''Are there any good people left out there?'' or ''Where are all the terrific people?'' I say, ''Take a close look.'' There are many terrific people right in front of our noses, and all too often we don't even realize it.

WHY YOU NEED TERRIFIC
PEOPLE IN YOUR LIFE

We need other people in our lives in order to survive. Without nurturing, infants die. Without the physical and emotional stimulation of another person, children disintegrate and may be headed toward mental, physical, and/or emotional retardation. They may begin to even engage in self-destructive behavior. We have seen the negative results of lack of stimulation most clearly with animals living in cages at the zoo. Deprived of their natural habitat or adequate socialization, these animals often pace back and forth in their small cages, pull out their fur or their feathers, or even become so withdrawn that they often sit isolated in a corner and starve themselves to death.

Classic studies done in orphanages in the 1930s demonstrated the power of touch, love, and nurturing. It was discovered that more babies who were left in their cribs with minimal or no stimulation died than those who were given more physical and emotional stimulation. Those who were taken out of their cribs regularly, played with, kissed, and hugged were healthier, more robust, and smiled more.

People need people in order to survive. The hungry would starve; the shivering would freeze; the person stuck in a flaming building would burn; and the person not rescued from a natural disaster would die if it weren't for other people there to help.

We not only need people to survive, but we need them to succeed.

Do you know the single most important secret of success in life? It is other people. The truth is that *everyone who attains true success in life does so only with the help and with the support of other people.*

People Need People!

No matter how talented or smart we are, none of us can make it to the top or achieve our goals by ourselves. We simply cannot do it alone, no matter what anyone may tell you to the contrary.

Dr. Robert J. Gorlin, my mentor at the University of Minnesota, recently featured in *American Health* magazine as one of the top physicians in the nation, put it very simply. Whenever someone would compliment him on how brilliant, eloquent, helpful, kindhearted, compassionate, or humane he was, he would reply humbly, "One is only as great as the shoulders they stand on. And I've been blessed to have stood on some pretty great shoulders in my day."

How right he was! John Donne's famous essay said, "No man is an island." The great Barbra Streisand's classic song puts it differently, but no less accurately: "People who need people are the luckiest people in the world."

These words rang so true to me. I realized this clearly on the day I attended the memorial service in Hollywood for my dear buddy Charlie Minor. As I surveyed the crowd of more than two thousand mourners, I realized that in the final analysis, it doesn't matter how rich or famous we are or whom we know. What really matters is how many lives we touch—how much we love others, and how much others love us.

As I thought about Charlie both during and after the services, I remembered his special qualities, ones that enabled him to touch the lives of so many. He was the type of person who always had an extra plate and extra food available to anyone he knew who didn't have anyone with whom to spend the holidays. A person who would converse warmly and openly with people, anywhere, at any time regardless of who they were, what their social position was, how they looked, or whether or not he knew them. A person who was able to create much love in others. A person so terrific that thousands were mourning the loss of his warm and wonderful presence.

Only a terrific person could garner such reactions from others. My buddy Charlie was such a person. Even though he clearly had his flaws, like everyone else, he was a terrific person in every sense of the word.

A terrific person is someone who makes others realize their own self-worth. They bring out the best in everyone they meet. We can attract terrific people like a Charlie Minor or a Dr. Robert Gorlin to our lives, and we all have it within us to be terrific to others. We all have it in us to be extraordinary, giving, positive, and life-enhancing, so that we bring happiness to nearly everyone with whom we come in contact. We also have it in us to keep such people in our lives.

People who recognize that they need people are indeed the "luckiest people in the world" because they realize they need other people not only for survival, but for love, friendship, intimacy, successful living, and much more.

WHY HAVE YOU SABOTAGED YOURSELF IN THE PAST BY PUSHING TERRIFIC PEOPLE OUT OF YOUR LIFE?

If your self-esteem is so low that you don't believe you are a terrific person yourself, you may well find yourself pushing other terrific people out of your life because you feel as though you don't deserve them. This can have long-lasting negative consequences, as the following example illustrates:

Sheri and Irene had been friends for a long time. Irene was always generous about listening to Sheri's problems, especially any difficulties she was having with her boyfriend. Irene knew that Sheri was in a "toxic" relationship, but was always supportive of her. Late one night, Sheri called Irene in tears about her boyfriend. Irene had an early meeting the next morning, but she put her concerns aside as she attempted to counsel Sheri over the phone. However, when Irene told Sheri that she felt she shouldn't remain in a relationship with a man who was cheating on her, Sheri lashed out at Irene, swearing at her and finally slamming down the phone in Irene's ear. Irene then realized Sheri was not capable of hearing the truth. She was also stunned that Sheri would treat her so badly. She decided that in order to protect her own mental health, she had to unplug Sheri from her life.

After two years, Sheri finally dumped her cheating boy-friend. She began thinking about Irene and how she had pushed this wonderful person out of her life. Eventually Sheri called Irene and said, "Irene, I know I've been a horrible friend. I was drunk and desperate that night, and that is why I spoke to you that way." Sheri was hoping for a reconciliation, but Irene told her gently, but firmly, that she had moved on with her life and didn't want anything to do with Sheri any longer. Although it was painful for Sheri to accept, she realized that she had to take responsibility for the consequences of her terrible treatment of Irene.

Like Sheri, if you don't feel good about yourself or suffer from feelings of unworthiness, there may come a time when you begin to sabotage your relationships with the terrific people in your life.

Feeling Inferior to the Terrific Person

Katy met an acquaintance of hers while waiting in line at the bank. Katy told Darla about her upcoming wedding and about the new position she was up for at her office. When her turn to see the bank teller came, just before Katy left the line, she said to Darla, "Now pray for me that I get that job."

To her dismay, Darla replied, "No, then you'll have every-thing—a husband and a great job—and I'll be jealous," as she chuckled to indicate that she was joking.

But there was no joke here. Darla was clearly jealous and envious of Katy, and she told her the truth. Instead of being empowered and motivated that good things in life were possible and good things could come Darla's way, too, she felt intimidated and threatened by Katy's good fortune, thereby sabotaging a potentially good friendship that could have been mutually supportive.

Unfortunately, too many people suffer from the "competitive" game, which leads to the "jealousy" game. This often manifests itself in sarcasm or in snide comments. Stay away from any players of those games.

The Groucho Marx Syndrome

Ted recently met Lila at a dinner party. He was as physically and mentally attracted to her as she was to him. They went out on a date and had a wonderful time. They laughed a lot and talked about their mutual interests. They walked through an outdoor shopping mall hand in hand and even shared kisses on the beach. During their regular telephone chats, they opened up and shared what was important to each of them. Ted began to discover that a friendship with Lila—let alone a relationship—was not to be taken lightly. She was a woman of substance and had a great deal of inner strength and moral fiber. Suddenly his calls to her began to dwindle until they were nonexistent. When Lila attempted to call Ted, he was rather cold and distant. For weeks, a depressed Lila beat herself up about what she did to cause Ted not to call. After one session in my office, she realized clearly that it had nothing to do with her. Ted had a pattern of "loving and leaving them." When Lila recalled to me Ted's mentioning that he broke up with his last girlfriend because she wanted to marry him, it became all too clear. Ted did not want anyone who wanted him. When Lila showed him that she liked him, that she cared, Ted ran the other way. Lila was lucky that she didn't spend more time and get more serious with Ted because the result could have been as devastating as a similar situation was for Gina.

Gina married Steve after an effusive courtship. He told her constantly how wonderful and fabulous she was, showered her with gifts, and tended to her every need. After she finally said yes to his proposal and married him, a completely different Steve emerged. Suddenly Gina could do no right. Steve was mean to her, picky, and short-tempered. After two weeks of his "toxic" behavior, the wedding was annulled. After going into therapy, Steve revealed to his therapist that he felt that

Gina wasn't so great after all. He noticed that before they married she was rather aloof and distant. But after he proposed, he found her to be more attentive. She bought him gifts and made his favorite meals. He felt that if she liked him so much, there must be something wrong with her.

Unfortunately, like Steve, Ted, and Darla, there are many people who don't like themselves enough and don't feel worthy of a terrific person in their life.

Ted, Steve, and Darla suffer from what is known as ''The Groucho Marx Syndrome.'' The late comedian Groucho Marx once joked that he wouldn't want to be a member of any club who would want him as a member.

Even though this was said in jest, there is nothing funny about people who feel that way about themselves. Feeling this way about oneself screams of insecurity, worthlessness, and even self-loathing. If you find yourself feeling this way at any time, it is in your best interest to consult a professional counselor or therapist who can address these issues and help you to overcome them so that you don't have to push away the wonderful people whom you are lucky enough to have in your life.

PEOPLE DESERVE TERRIFIC PEOPLE IN THEIR LIVES, BUT FOR SOME IT'S OVERWHELMING

Although you may long intellectually and emotionally for nothing more than to have your life filled with terrific people, you may have found that your most precious relationships have too often been marred by conflict and misunderstanding. Why is it that all too often after a person has encountered a terrific person they go out of their way to sabotage the potential friendship or current relationship? Oftentimes it is because they don't feel that they deserve terrific people in their lives because they don't feel so ''terrific'' about themselves. Hidden hang-ups may lead one to sabotage potentially wonderful relationships with harmful behaviors such as running the other way, saying mean things, or otherwise behaving badly.

There are a number of reasons for these negative actions. For example, some may feel inferior around terrific people. Others may feel so unworthy that they can't comprehend why a terrific person would actually want to be around them, let alone like them. Still others may feel that the terrific person is out of their league, that they would make fun of them or belittle them behind their back, try to control them, or eventually reject them.

They Are Not in My League

Neil was a house painter who was eking out a living. The recent rains left his business dry, so he was extremely diligent when he got a job painting Laurie's house. He worked hard and paid attention to every detail. When Laurie came home after a long day at work, he would ask if he could help her with anything around the house or do any errands for her. Neil was so attentive and kind to Laurie who encountered so many "toxic" people in her daily activities as an attorney, that she welcomed and appreciated Neil in her life. After the painting job was over, Laurie wanted to keep him around, so she created more jobs for him. Eventually their mutual attraction for each other surfaced, and Neil moved into Laurie's home, all the while telling himself that he was "out of her league." After all, he thought, Laurie was a successful, high-powered, highly educated professional. What did she want with a bum who had quit high school, had a reading disorder, didn't know the right words to use, let alone the right utensils with which to eat?

Although Laurie didn't seem to mind the mismatch, Neil did. He let her know it constantly. At first he made subtle negative remarks about Laurie; then he resorted to full-blown open hostility toward her. Because he felt he was "out of her league,'' she made certain that he was "out of her league" forever—by throwing him out of her home and out of her life.

They May Try to Belittle or Control Me

All too often, when people don't feel that they deserve to have a terrific person in their lives, they often project their own paranoia and insecurities onto that terrific person. They misinterpret the person's inner strength and self-esteem as an attempt to control them. Often, people who feel that way have such little control over their own lives that when they see someone assert themselves or take charge, they immediately feel that the person is trying to overpower them.

Linda was a seamstress who was new in town. Gloria, a very wealthy and prominent socialite who went to her for some alterations noticed that not only did Linda do a good job, she was very sweet, soft-spoken, and highly accommodating. As a result, Gloria sent everyone she knew to Linda for their alterations. As a result, Linda's business grew exponentially.

One day Gloria called Linda up to do a rush job; she had a very important event to attend and needed the dress in two days. Linda snapped, "Look, stop trying to control me. I just can't jump to your beck and call. I'm not a trained seal who jumps through hoops at your every command." Gloria was flabbergasted. She had spoken to Linda only with kindness, had gone out of her way to send her clients, and had even brought her cut flowers from her garden regularly. She had no idea where Linda's venom was coming from. Linda's venom and her irrational lashing out came from the fact that she was out of control in her own life, from her finances to her overeating to her lack of time. She projected her insecurity and paranoia at not being able to control her own life onto Gloria. Her comment about not wanting to be "controlled" by Gloria was made because she was jealous of Gloria's self-confidence, assertiveness, and her power—the same power that built Linda's business. She felt irrationally that if Gloria had so much control, she might try to control Linda's life as well.

They Might Reject Me

Unfortunately, people who suffer from low self-esteem and don't feel as though they are worthy of having terrific people in their lives will often reject the very person they want to be around the most, for fear that the person will "get wise" to them and reject them first. In order not to get hurt by the rejection, they will often sabotage the relationship by finding some flaw in the person so as not to be rejected first.

Margo was involved in a terrible car accident that left her with two broken legs. Her terrific friend Lisa was there for her nearly twenty-four hours a day. Although Margo realized what a dedicated friend Lisa was, sacrificing her time by putting her own life on hold in order to help Margo, Margo was a horrible patient. She refused to obey the doctors' orders, felt terribly sorry for herself, and even threatened suicide. Feeling helpless, Lisa firmly told Margo that she didn't want to hear any more talk of suicide and that if Margo was considering it seriously, she would call the local hospital and have her committed. Embarrassed by her behavior and frightened that Lisa might get so fed up with her that she would walk out, thereby leaving her helpless, she wanted to "beat Lisa to the punch" and reject her first by finding fault with whatever Lisa did to help her.

Because Margo kept obsessing over her old boyfriend Greg's not calling her, well-meaning Lisa took it upon herself to call and tell Greg about what had happened to Margo. When Margo found out, she now found the perfect reason to eject Lisa from her life before Lisa rejected her. She welcomed the opportunity to throw Lisa out of her home, insisting that she never speak to her again. After several attempts on Lisa's part to rectify the situation and to rekindle their friendship, Margo maintained her position as the "rejecter" by changing and unlisting her phone number and refusing to have anything to do with Lisa.

Unfortunately, this concept is all too familiar among people in the dating world. Often, if a man or a woman feels unworthy of the people they are with, they will reject them first, so they will have less heartache than if they are the rejected.

WARNING SIGNS OF UNWORTHINESS

If you find yourself having the following feelings or engaging in the following behaviors, you need to pay close attention to them. Your thoughts and actions may speak volumes in terms of how you really feel about yourself.

1. Feelings of jealousy toward the terrific person.

2. Tuning out and not respecting what terrific people say or the advice they give you.

3. "Forgetting" to return phone calls or arriving late for appointments.

4. Feeling irritated with or annoyed by minor things the person does.

5. Feeling as if you want to attack the other person verbally.

You may wonder why we often treat the people who are best to us worse than we treat anyone else. The answer is simple: because we have terrible feelings of unworthiness about ourselves. We envy these people, which means we unconsciously want to sabotage or destroy them because we don't feel we deserve them.

STEPS TO KEEP YOURSELF FROM SABOTAGING YOUR PRECIOUS RELATIONSHIPS

If you begin to notice feelings of inadequacy and toxic behavior in yourself, here are some valuable steps you can take in order to keep yourself from sabotaging the precious relationships in your life:

1. Focus your attention on the problem. For example, why can't you stand your neighbor, or why does your co-worker drive you up the wall? Why do these people have such a negative effect on you? Bring it to your awareness because knowledge is power. Awareness of your feelings of jealousy or inadequacy often gives you the power to change your feelings and behavior.

2. You may find it helpful to take some personal time to go off by yourself, sit down, and list all the great things the person has done for you. It may be helpful to keep a journal where you write your thoughts, feelings, and insights as you read this book and again after you finish reading it.

3. Do something unexpected or thoughtful for that person. Show him you are thinking of him and let him know how much you appreciate his presence in your life.

4. Sit down and give yourself a serious "self-talk" about the possible consequences of alienating this "terrific person"—and potentially losing him. Because of your actions, there may be no going back.

Your family may love you unconditionally, but your friends—even the terrific ones—are under no such obligation. If you push them too far, you will be sure to end up as Sheri did, regretting having lost a terrific person from your life.

OVERCOMING YOUR FEARS

Fear is the mortal enemy of having terrific relationships with terrific people. It is the root of why people sabotage themselves and jeopardize friendships and life-enhancing experiences with others.

As President Franklin D. Roosevelt put it so eloquently, ''There is nothing to fear but fear itself.'' How right he was. Often all it takes to get over our fears is to acknowledge their existence and then positively talk ourselves out of being afraid.

Based on my years of experience treating clients, I am a firm believer that knowledge is power. If you know what you are doing wrong and why you are doing it, then you have the power to change it.

For example, if you know that you haven't had many terrific people in your life because you feel insecure or inadequate around them, and that when you are around them you may act out in ways that are not conducive toward maintaining a relationship, you may want to be mindful of what people and situations provoke these feelings of inadequacy. Stop yourself, leave the room if you have to, and give yourself a pep talk. Tell yourself that you are worthy of having these people in your life, you deserve them, and that you are a better person for knowing them, just as they are better for knowing you. If you don't believe it, say it again and again. Say it out loud. Say it as you look into a mirror. Say it as though you mean it—and you will find that you do. Once and for all, break the pattern of feeling unworthy around that person or event. Remind yourself of things you have done that have enriched that person's life. If you can't think of anything, think of what you could and will do. Once again, say it out loud. Each time repeat to yourself that you are worthy and you deserve to have people like____in your life. Then go out there and in your kindest, most positive tone, say something positive to him or her. And don't forget to tell these people how much you appreciate having them in your life.

YOU DESERVE THE BEST THAT PEOPLE HAVE TO OFFER

Only after you acknowledge your fears, confront your inner demons of unworthiness, and exorcise all of the wrong information that has been programmed in you by toxic people who previously have infected your life, can you feel that you deserve the best that people have to offer.

Every human being has the right to be treated with respect and dignity, to be spoken to kindly and gently, to be encouraged, supported, and given a chance to be the best person possible. When we treat one another with love, respect, and kindness, we grow, we blossom, we reach over the top, and we excel.

When we aren't nurtured or supported, the reverse happens. We wither; we shrink; we die. Human beings are fragile; they are sensitive and delicate. If they are not treated with love and kindness, they cannot function optimally. Look at what happens when people aren't nourished with kindness early in their lives. The results are so devastating that many middle-aged adults continue to seek the services of trained therapists and counselors to help them rid themselves of the emptiness and the excruciating pain of not having had enough terrific people around in their formative years to nurture them emotionally.

Even if you were abused as a child or a young adult, you don't have to continue this horrible cycle. You can heal yourself—and the wounds of the past—by surrounding yourself with those people who tell you how terrific you are and who show you so by their actions. To meet Glenda, one would never know that she was a victim of severe child abuse. All through her twenties, she was drawn to people who continued to abuse her physically, mentally, and emotionally. I treated my client, Glenda, with the same love, kindness, and respect with which I treat my other clients. I was supportive and nurturing and encouraged her to be a better communicator by verbalizing her needs and wants, instead of expecting people to be mind readers and then getting disappointed when they didn't do what she expected of them. One day she came into my office in tears and handed me the following note, which she wanted me to read in front of her:

You know, Dr. Glass, every time I have come into your office, you always greet me with a smile. You have a sparkle in your eyes and a bounce in your voice whenever you talk to me. You listen to everything I tell you, all of my problems. You give me the right advice and you have repeatedly shown me that you care about me. You have even gone out of your way to refer me to certain doctors, to hook me up with the right accountant, and you have even introduced me to someone who hired me for a job that I always wanted. You continue to build up my self-esteem by always telling me how good I look and sound. You are genuinely happy and excited for me when things go my way in my career and with my personal life. Whenever I leave your office, you never fail to stand up and give me a hug. Dr. Glass, this is the first time in my life that anyone has made me feel like a worthwhile human being. You have shown me how I must be treated the rest of my life and how I must treat others. I will accept nothing less from anyone. I will never forget you because you have given me the greatest gift that no amount of money could possibly buy: my dignity and self-worth. May God always bless you and allow you to continue your great work so that you can touch other people's lives the way you touched mine.

This woman's letter moved me to tears as I reflected on my own life. She, too, had given me the best possible gift—that of allowing me to enrich her life so that she could go on and enrich the lives of others. I felt that she was worth it, and she, in turn, felt that I was worth it. All of us are worth nothing less than to have terrific people in our lives who open our hearts and touch our souls.

WHAT KNOWING TERRIFIC PEOPLE CAN DO FOR YOU

The central theme of this book is "people finding happiness through helping others." Finding terrific people to enhance your life can help you: to eliminate loneliness; reduce and even eliminate certain forms of depression; enhance your social life; find a better job; rise up the ladder of success at greater speed; and have a more fun-filled, exciting life.

No More Loneliness

How often have you sat at home alone with all the energy in the world, ready to go somewhere or do something but having nobody to do it with? You may have even gone so far as picking up the phone to dial a number, only to discover that you have no one to call. Suddenly you experience that sick feeling in the pit of your stomach. You feel awful, embarrassed, and sad that there is nobody in your life whom you can pick up the phone to call, who will be there for you.

If you have ever experienced loneliness—the painful realization of not having people in your life whom you need—you are not alone. Most of us have experienced it at one time or another. Single people and teenagers are most prone to loneliness. Surveys have shown that at least 50 percent of single people find loneliness to be the worst part of being single. Surveys have also reported that over 20 percent of American teenagers feel "terribly lonely." Even if you have a spouse or you are living with a household of people, you can still be lonely if you are not with the right people.

When you are with a terrific person with whom you are harmonious, you don't experience loneliness. You also experience better physical and mental health. In fact, studies have shown that people who are lonely tend to have more alcohol- and drug-related health problems, and a higher incidence of heart disease.

Reduce or Eliminate Depression

While recent research has shown that there is a large biochemical component in incidences of clinical depression, there are many studies that have correlated depression to loneliness. Thus, when we are around terrific people who make us smile, laugh, and stimulate our interest, who accept us for who we are, and who make us feel good about ourselves, it's pretty difficult to feel depressed around them.

Even though Connie had a great job and a great home, she seemed to be depressed quite often. She went from therapist to therapist looking for a cure. She described herself as feeling apathetic, bored, negative, unhappy, and alienated. No therapist seemed to help her and no drug seemed to work. As a last resort, after having read *Toxic People,* she contacted me. After extensive communication, we found out that the root of her problem was that she felt as though she could not relate to many people on the West Coast, where she had moved recently from New York. She had a better job and made a lot more money, but she was still miserable. I encouraged her to try to find work back on the East Coast. Even though it might mean less money, she would be around more people to whom she felt she could relate. She took my advice and has never been happier. She goes out every night, has found numerous terrific girlfriends with whom to go to dinner, theater, and to the movies. She also recently met a terrific man whom she may marry.

All it took for Connie to get over her depression was to be around some terrific people to whom she could relate.

Whether you live on the East Coast or the West Coast or the Mid West, there are terrific people everywhere. Unlike Connie, most people can't afford to relocate. Most people "take themselves wherever they go," and therefore need to be happy with themselves, wherever they may be.

Enhance Your Social Life

As human beings, we need a lot of stimulation. We need people with whom we can share ideas and with whom we can express our innermost feelings. As we attract one or two terrific people into our lives, they often know other terrific people, to whom they will introduce us who know other terrific people to whom they will introduce us. And thus the social cycle begins.

When Janet moved to Chicago, she knew only Vivien, who invited her to a tea she was giving for twenty women. At the tea, Janet met all of Vivien's friends, but really connected with five people. Janet took their cards and then had lunch with each of the five women, two of whom she felt she could really relate to. Those two women, Elaine and Candy, became close friends and invited her to parties and social functions. At those social functions, she met new people with whom she connected. Eventually Janet became one of the most social women in Chicago. Because she wasn't married, her newfound friends would often invite her to dinner parties and seat her next to an eligible bachelor. On one occasion she was seated next to a man who turned out to have so much in common with her that she ended up marrying him.

In essence, Janet was able to meet her husband because her social life increased. It started by meeting one terrific woman, Vivien, and then other terrific women at the tea, who knew other terrific people, who knew other terrific people, and so on and so forth.

As we have seen in Janet's case, one social encounter has the potential to make you one of the most popular and socially-sought-after individuals.

Get a Better Job

Most of the best job opportunities are not listed in the news-papers. Instead, they are listed in the minds and in the mouths of other people. All too often, someone may be working for a company or have a friend working at another company who hears about a particular job that might be just perfect for you. If you associate with terrific people who tend to keep others in mind, they will often let you know about these opportunities. This is called "networking."

After being laid off from her job because of downsizing, Cindy was unemployed for six months. Jennifer tried to be supportive by listening to her dilemma, but couldn't offer Cindy any tangible leads for a specific job in her field. She could only be a good listener to a friend in need. One day Jennifer met a friend of hers for lunch, who brought her sister Kim along. Kim told Jennifer how she had a catering business that was growing by leaps and bounds, and that she needed to find some great help. Her assistant, who was responsible for the bookings and organizing the catering staff, had quit, and she was overwhelmed with the workload. She wanted to find a stable, highly organized person with a lot of patience, who knew how to speak to customers, handle crises, and who would also be willing to be a server at events, if need be. Just as she was describing her ideal assistant, Jennifer thought of Cindy. Even though Cindy knew nothing about the food business ex-cept that she liked to eat, Jennifer knew that she would be perfect because she possessed all of the traits Kim was looking for. Now Cindy has a job because her terrific friend Jennifer hooked her up with Kim. Had it not been for Jennifer, Cindy might still be unemployed.

Rising Up the Ladder of Success

Even though we would like to think that with a lot of hard work, diligence, and patience, we can reach the top of our field, the truth is that we may be struggling and waiting to get there until we are ready to retire. In order to make it to the top a lot faster, you need terrific people to help you climb the rungs of the ladder. Even though it may not seem fair or democratic, it is a reality.

Carla worked for a major cosmetics company in middle management for thirteen years. Even though she was great at what she did, she never could rise above a certain position in her company—until she met Ken, the CEO of a major company, who also happened to be best friends with Marvin, the CEO of Carla's firm. After meeting with Marvin, who was impressed with her background, qualifications, knowledge, and business savvy, within days, Carla was promoted to an executive position.

Similarly, a well-known actor client of mine couldn't get arrested in Hollywood. Even though he took every acting class and workshop, went to every open audition, went to the gym every day, had a great body, the right Hollywood look, a great voice, and the right clothes, he couldn't get a role, let alone an agent. After knocking on hundreds of doors, and leaving his photo and résumé in different agents' offices and not getting any responses, he was beside himself as to what it took to make it in Hollywood.

What it took was other people who believed in him as much as he believed in himself.

One night in his acting class, Julie, a classmate, congratulated him on his performance of a touching monologue by telling him what a great actor she thought he was. He chuckled and said, "I sure wish an agent felt the same way you did." Julie, a working actress, agreed to introduce him to her agent. He and the agent hit it off. The rest is history. Today, you see him constantly in major films.

More Fun and Excitement in Your Life

Somehow life seems like more fun just by hanging out with a terrific person. New adventures and new experiences mean an entirely new life. While watching a frustrated woman struggling to set the controls for the treadmill at the gym, Denise walked over to the woman and showed her how to use the equipment. As a result, they got to know one another and had great chats at the gym. Ruth found Denise to be a terrific person, unlike many of the people in her social arena. Denise was so open, real, and genuine that Ruth enjoyed being around her. Denise, on the other hand, loved talking to Ruth because she found her to be polished and sophisticated. One day Ruth invited Denise to a cocktail party she was giving at her home, which turned out to be a huge mansion in Beverly Hills, complete with uniformed maids and butlers. Some of the most famous people in the world were at the party, from society women to movie stars, television talk-show hosts to business tycoons, from film producers to senators. Denise was floored that Ruth actually knew and associated with the very people Denise idolized and dreamed to be around.

Being friends with Ruth opened up a whole new world of fun and excitement for Denise, which included trips to the Cannes Film Festival, Morocco, shopping sprees in Italy, black-tie galas in Washington D.C., a trip to the White House, court-side seats at the Lakers games, the Kentucky Derby, Monaco, and Ascot, dinner parties attended by members of the British royal family, and sharing laughs and flirtation with some of the sexiest and most powerful men in the world. It also gave her the opportunity to learn exciting new things—to understand the art world, horses, fashion, and much more. Her exposure to these interesting and wonderful people changed her life forever.

Although Denise's experience is rather extreme—a Cinderella story, if you will—she also changed the course of Ruth's life. Ruth found Denise's enthusiasm and zest for life refreshing. She loved her honesty and respected her integrity and values. Through Denise's viewpoint, Ruth was able to see all of the wonderful things she had and places she had access to in a brand-new, and exciting, light. She had a newfound appreciation for not only what she had, but who she was. For the first time in Ruth's life, she actually enjoyed herself and appreciated the fact that she had the financial means to take advantage of what she was lucky enough to do.

UNLIKE THE EXTREME case of Denise and Ruth, on a smaller scale, just meeting a terrific person with whom you click can make a simple experience of going to see a movie one of the most exciting, energizing, and fun-filled experiences you have ever had.

Associating with terrific people who have unique and different interests, lifestyles, or even life views allows you to enter their worlds and experience life through others' perspectives. It opens up life's possibilities—and rewards.

Who Are the Terrific People in Your Life?

*𝒯*n this chapter you will learn how to identify the traits of terrific people. The Terrific People Quiz will help you to look at your own emotional, behavioral, physical, and communication responses to the people in your life, and you may discover who is terrific for you.

Are there enough terrific people in your life now? Take this quiz and find out. As you read through these questions, think about your spontaneous responses to the people in your life. Do you know someone in particular about whom you would answer ''yes'' to most or all of these questions? After you're done, read the comments at the end of the quiz to find out what your responses indicate about the people in your life.

TERRIFIC PEOPLE QUIZ

Emotional Reactions

1. Do you feel excited and energized after talking to or being with this person?

2. Are you in a great mood when you are around the person?

3. Deep down, do you really like the person and do you feel he or she likes you?

4. Do you come away feeling confident after being around the person?

5. Does the person make you feel great, attractive, intelligent, respected, and worthy?

6. Do you feel empty, as if something is missing, when you are away from this person?

7. Do you feel safe and secure around the person?

8. Do you always feel like laughing or smiling whenever you are with the person, or whenever you think of him or her?

9. Does the person involve you when he or she is around others and sing your praises?

10. Do you feel that the person has no feelings of jealousy, envy, or competitiveness toward you?

Behavioral Reactions

1. Do you find that you are more motivated to do things after being around the person?

2. Does the person bring out the very best behavior in you?

3. Do you have the urge to hug, kiss, touch, and show affection freely to the person?

4. Are your affections reciprocated?

5. Do you act naturally and comfortably around the person?

6. Is the person genuinely concerned about you, your feelings, and your thoughts—and does he or she show it?

7. Is the person honest with you, and do you feel that you can be open and honest with him or her without feeling ridiculed or judged?

8. Does the person unselfishly go out of their way for you or try to please you?

9. Is the person generous with you?

10. Do you feel that you smile more and look your best whenever you are around that person?

Communication Reactions

1. Does the person usually say kind things about you and about others?

2. Would the person support or defend you verbally if someone said something negative about you, and vice versa?

3. Does the person often use terms of politeness and terms of endearment when speaking with you?

4. Is the person mostly complimentary, telling you what you are doing "right" as opposed to telling you what you are doing "wrong"?

5. Do you speak to one another in kind and loving tones?

6. Is the person consistent in the positive things that they say to you?

7. Do you respect what each other has to say, and do you feel as though the person is really listening to you?

8. Do you find that you always have enough to say to each other and that you can talk for long periods of time without getting bored or feeling uninterested?

9. Do you speak to each other in enthusiastic, upbeat tones? Are you excited when you first hear the sound of each other's voice? Do you have a pleasant expression on your face when you speak to each other?

10. Do you speak to each other openly and honestly with respect, and never would think of using bad or abusive language to each other?

Physical Reactions

1. Do you feel more alert and alive after being around the person?

2. Do you feel that this person also has the ability to calm you down so that you don't feel stressed out and tense?

3. Do you like the way the person looks, dresses, sounds, and smells?

4. Do you like the way the person touches you?

5. Is the person action-oriented, and does he or she do things on your behalf?

6. Would you protect the person physically and would he or she protect you if it was necessary?

7. Do you feel great physical excitement when you are around the person—does your heart beat faster, and do you feel happier?

8. Is it difficult for you to leave the person after you have been together?

9. Do you do things together and share similar activities?

10. Do you find that you actually look better when you are around the person or have been around the person recently?

WHAT YOUR RESPONSES MEAN

If you answered ''yes'' to most of these questions, you are fortunate indeed! You have a relationship with at least one terrific person who enhances your self-esteem and makes you feel good about yourself physically, emotionally, and mentally by bringing out the best in you and thereby allowing you to bring out the best in yourself. If you answered "yes" to half of the questions, you are still in good shape and may want to expand your horizons to meet even more terrific people. But if you realized that after taking this quiz, you have very few terrific people in your life—or perhaps none at all—don't worry!

As you read this book, you will learn how to attract more terrific people into your life. You will also learn how to become an even more terrific person yourself—which will further help you to attract more and more terrific people to you, in an ever-expanding spiral of joy and fulfillment.

WHO IS TERRIFIC FOR YOU?

Just as there are "toxic people" you have met throughout your life for whom you did not particularly care, who had traits and characteristics that nearly drove you up the wall or brought out the worst in you, there are terrific people who bring out the very best in you. If you consider the specific personality traits you find attractive in people, it won't surprise you that the people you hold dearest to your heart are the ones who share similar traits. The traits that you find appealing in women may differ from those you find appealing in men, as I, too, discovered while doing the following exercise:

Who Is Terrific For You?

1. List five men and five women whom you have admired and respected throughout the years. Reflect on everyone who has been in your life from childhood to the present, and include them in your list.

2. Think about why you like or even love these people. Next to their names, list several positive characteristics that best describe their personality traits. If you are stuck, here is a list of words to help you describe some of their positive characteristics:

PERSONALITY CHARACTERISTICS OF TERRIFIC PEOPLE:
THEY ARE . . . THEY DO . . . THEY HAVE . . . THEY WILL . . .

accepting
accommodating
accomplished
active
admits to mistakes
affectionate
alert
alive
ambitious
animated
appealing
appreciative
approachable
assertive
attractive
aware of others
backbone
balanced
bold
brave
bright
brilliant
bubbly
calculated-risk
  taker
calm
calming
caring
centered
charismatic
charming
chatty

childlike
classy
clean
clearheaded
clever
comprehensible
committed
communicative
compassionate
concerned
confident
confront
  appropriately
connected
conscious
consistent
creative
credible
curious
daring
decisive
deep
definite
deliberate
delightful
demonstrative
democratic
discerning
diverse
down-to-earth
easygoing
easy to talk to

educated
educating
elegant
emotive
emotional
energetic
enterprising
enlightening
enthusiastic
entreprenurial
even-tempered
evolved
exacting
exciting
expressive
fair
fastidious
fearless
feminine
flexible
focused
forceful when
  needed
friendly
full of life
fun-loving
forthright
generous
genuine
giving
goal-oriented
good-natured

gracious
grateful
gregarious
guiltless
happy
hardworking
healthy
helpful
honorable
honest
humble
humorous
imaginative
independent
inner-directed
inner strength
innocent
innovative
interested
integrity
in the moment
joker
joyful
kind
knowledgeable
laughing
law-abiding
leader
learns from
  mistakes
levelheaded
likes himself/herself
limitless
listens well
lively
loving
loyal

manly
masculine
mature
meditative
modern
moral
motivating
nonabusive
noncompetitive
noncritical
nonviolent
not adversarial
not aggressive
not blaming
not complaining
not defensive
not destructive
not gossiping
not guilt ridden
not frightened
not invasive
not jealous
not judgmental
not self-destructive
not self-righteous
not threatening
not troubled
not victimlike
nurturing
old-fashioned
open emotionally
open-minded
open up
optimistic
organized
orderly
outgoing

passionate
patient
people person
personable
plan ahead
playful
predictable
positive
proactive
prominent
protective
proud
provocative
quick-witted
quiet
rational
real
realistic
reasonable
religious
reputable
respectable
respectful
responsible
satisfied
satisfiable
secure
self-assured
self-esteem
selfless
self-motivated
self-worth
sense of humor
sensitive
sensual
sensuous
serious

sexual	*trusting*	*verbal*
simple	*trustworthy*	*vulnerable*
smart	*truthful*	*warm*
sober	*unafraid*	*well-balanced*
socially aware	*unashamed*	*well-groomed*
soft	*uncomplicated*	*well-learned*
soft-spoken	*uncowardly*	*well-mannered*
spiritual	*understanding*	*well-read*
straightforward	*uninhibited*	*well-respected*
strong	*unintimidated*	*well-rounded*
studious	*unintimidating*	*well-spoken*
successful	*unpretentious*	*willing*
sunny	*unrepressed*	*winner*
sweet	*unselfish*	*wise*
talented	*unsuspicious*	*witty*
talkative	*untroubled*	*worthy*
tenacious	*upbeat*	*zealous*
tender	*up-front*	*Zen-like*
thoughtful	*values*	*zest for life*

3. Now, compare your list of traits and see how many positive traits each of the people whom you respect and admire have in common. You will be as intrigued as I was to see how many positive traits are shared by these particular terrific people on your list.

I discovered that I tend to gravitate toward dynamic, energetic, and creative women, whereas I am drawn mostly to even-tempered, good-natured, kind, successful, and enterprising men.

This exercise will be most helpful in enabling you to determine, quickly and painlessly, how compatible you will be with someone and how close and what role they should play in your life. The margin of error is very small in terms of making a mistake and letting the wrong person into your life because you can look at his or her characteristics more objectively and realistically in terms of how you will best fit together. That does not mean that you cannot love, accept, and appreciate those who don't fall into your list of preferred characteristics. However, there is a greater chance of getting along with less stress and with greater understanding if they do possess these traits, and of a more harmonious and longer-lasting relationship.

This technique changed the quality of many of my clients' lives. For example, before doing this exercise, Larissa, a single, beautiful, accomplished clothing designer and manufacturer complained constantly that she was a "jerk magnet." She said that all the men she dated and ended up getting involved with constantly put her down, always telling her what was wrong with her, rather than what was right.

Initially, these men would build her up and be so nice to her, and then, later in the relationship, they would become highly critical of whatever she said or did. She was ready to give up on men forever.

After doing this exercise, she discovered that the men in her life with whom she did get along were generally more successful than she was. They tended to be more mature men who were impressed—not threatened—by her spunk and aggressiveness.

It was as though a light went off in Larissa's head as she realized that all the men she had gotten involved with were troubled, financially unstable, hated their jobs, and were about her age. Because they were so miserable in their own lives, they couldn't stand her being so happy in her career. Therefore, in their attempts to push her off her pedestal by putting her down, they attempted to make her feel as insecure about herself as they were about themselves. As a result, she recently met a man at a party who was nothing like the previous men she dated, but rather like men friends and colleagues with whom she tended to get along. Today she is happily married to that man and is expecting her first baby at age forty-two.

Similarly, Georgette also experienced much pain and disappointment, but mostly through the jealousy and envy of other women. They often sabotaged her efforts or put her down. After realizing through the exercise that the women she would be most suited to have as friends would be nonvictim-like, self-sufficient, independent, and accomplished women, it came as no surprise that her "new best friend," Martha, should never have been relegated to the position of "best friend" in the first place.

Georgette was already an accomplished songwriter with a national reputation when she first moved to Nashville. Martha was a struggling singer who couldn't get—much less keep— a waitress job. She had no money and always seemed to be involved in one crisis after another. Through her contacts, Georgette tried to help her newfound friend get some auditions. When a contact was out of town or had agreed to see Martha in two weeks, Martha became short with Georgette, as though it was her fault that the meeting wasn't happening fast enough. Georgette gave her friend a part-time job making public-relations calls for her. To her great embarrassment, Martha would reveal her personal sordid past to these business contacts. Obviously, this reflected poorly on Georgette.

After doing the exercise, Georgette got all of the victimlike, jealous, Martha types out of her life. She made it a policy to never again pick up "stray dogs" who were bound to "bite her" in the end, just as Martha did. Now she is highly selective with her women friends and allows only other competent women into her life. As a result, she has never had so much fun or such easygoing and solid relationships with women friends in her life.

When you are with the people whose traits suit you best, you will find that relationships are easy. They flow. You understand one another so much better. There is no hidden agenda or inner hostility. These equal relationships lend themselves to open, honest communication so that you can quickly work out any problems that may arise.

THE "ASSOCIATIVE PROPERTY" OF TERRIFIC PEOPLE MEETING OTHER TERRIFIC PEOPLE

Do you remember back in high-school algebra when you learned about the associative property? You may even have wondered, "How is knowing this ever going to help me in life?" or "When will I ever use this information again?"

Well, here is what you have been waiting for. It is called the Associative Property of Friendship. To refresh your memory, the associative property states that if "a" is equal to "b" and "b" is equal to "c," then "a" is equal to "c." Now let's apply this concept to the topic of terrific people. If terrific person Ann likes terrific person Barbara likes terrific person Carol, then most likely Ann will like Carol. Since Ann shares so many similar traits with Barbara, thereby making them good friends, and since Barbara shares so many terrific traits with Carol, then it stands to reason that Ann and Carol would share similar terrific traits and would have a lot in common, thereby potentially making them dear friends as well.

This is why, when terrific people introduce terrific friends who have similar traits in common, new friendships occur almost immediately. This is what happened to my friends Bev and Carla. I absolutely adore Bev for all the reasons I listed in the "Who Is Terrific for You?" exercise. I adore my friend Carla for similar reasons that I adore Bev. When I introduced Bev to Carla, they both clicked instantly and now are the dearest of friends. If two terrific best friends don't click, it may be because the friends don't have terrific traits in common, or there may be jealousy or competitiveness.

THE SPIRAL OF TERRIFIC PEOPLE—
PEOPLE HELPING OTHER PEOPLE

We have all heard the expression, "Birds of a feather flock together." This is especially true in terms of terrific people. If you begin to associate only with terrific people, you will start to meet other terrific people through them. Eventually, as you begin to meet the friends of your terrific friends, you will come to see that not only will they get along, but that these terrific people's friends will know other terrific people. Thus an entire network of terrific people is formed. This is called "The Spiral of Friendship." The more terrific people with whom you connect, the more terrific people you meet, and the spiral continues on and on.

Out of this spiral come incredible friendships, which are real, nonsuperficial, long-lasting, supportive, uplifting, helpful, and life-enhancing. In this spiral, people will help one another achieve what they need or want, whether they are business, personal, or even love contacts.

This happened to me when I moved to New York City. I hardly knew anyone when I came to the city, with the exception of some people in the media business and a few former clients with whom I had worked back in Los Angeles. Before I moved to New York, my friend Arnold Kopelson introduced me to his terrific friends in New York, Nat and Vivien Serota. Vivien introduced me to her friend Helene Kaplan, who was also a friend of Arnold Kopelson. Helene told her friend Peter that I was moving to New York and needed a place to live. Out of the blue, I received a call at my hotel one morning from Peter Levine, who introduced me to one of the most reputable realtors in Manhattan, who showed me the perfect apartment in the perfect area, for the perfect price, which I rented on the spot. Thus, I had a nice place to live.

Upon arriving in New York, Vivien Serota introduced me to Diane Felenstein, who then became my dear friend, who introduced me to her terrific friend Carol Levin, who introduced me to her husband, Jerry Levin, CEO of Revlon, who introduced me to a business contact of his.

Meanwhile, my close friend, Dana Lowey, introduced me to her mother, United States Congresswoman Nita Lowey. Hence, I was invited to a political fund-raiser for Nita Lowey given by Hillary Clinton. There I ran into Diane Felenstein, who knew Nita Lowey, and to Sheila Grant, another lovely friend I met recently. I discovered that Sheila and Diane knew each other. Sheila then told me that she knew a nice gentleman whom she thought I should meet.

As you can see by my own experience, the Spiral of Friendship grew and grew and is continuing to grow as I meet more and more terrific people through other terrific people.

When you collect and associate only with terrific people, no matter how few they are to start out with, after a period of time you will notice that more and more great people will come into your life. These people will open doors for you and will open a whole new world for you financially, socially, intellectually, emotionally, spiritually, and culturally.

This happened to Edith Weiner, one of the leading futurists and strategic thinkers in the world and one of the founders of Weiner, Edrich, Brown, a firm that analyzes emerging trends for major corporations. At the age of twenty-seven she started her own research firm, and at the age of twenty-eight sat on the board of directors of a major Fortune 500 company.

Several years ago, this beautiful, classy, brilliant, dynamic, and accomplished woman decided that she did not know enough women like herself, so she set forth to meet and befriend other women by using the Spiral of Friendship concept. She met a powerful woman in the fashion industry who ended up introducing her to other powerful women, who introduced her to . . . and the cycle continued. As a result, Edith has not only enriched her life with new, incredibly wonderful friends, sitting on additional boards of directors of many other major companies and associations, but was recently invited to the White House, where she sat next to the Secretary of State and the President of Mexico. She is now one of the most influential women in New York.

Because of her incredible, high-powered women friendships, everyone she knows refers to her connections as ''Edith's Mafia.'' About six years ago, Edith decided to put her ''Mafia'' to work for a good cause and brought over 500 phenomenal women together in an awards ceremony to honor Linda Ellerbee, Lena Horne, and others. The purpose of her event was to raise money for a mentoring program for young inner-city girls, so that they could have the exposure, contact, and opportunities to enhance their futures. By pairing them up with accomplished terrific women, who are their mentors, these young girls are now open to new opportunities that could set them on a winning course for the rest of their lives.

''IN-VISIONING'' THE TERRIFIC PEOPLE YOU WOULD LIKE TO HAVE IN YOUR LIFE

Just as Edith Weiner created a life filled with many terrific people, you can and must do the same. You must actually see yourself having and deserving these phenomenal people in your life.

After I wrote *Toxic People* several years ago, I made the conscious decision to never have anyone in my life who wasn't terrific. I no longer wanted people in my personal life who were filled with negativity and who were always involved in one disaster after another. I did not want to be ''Dr. Glass'' in my personal relationships with others ever again; it was too draining, too frustrating, and too debilitating. Instead, I wanted to be Dr. Glass only when I was dealing with people on a professional level, during my working hours. Therefore, I made a conscious decision to attract only terrific people, people who were growers, people whose traits I truly admired and respected.

To ''in-vision'' these terrific people in your life, close your eyes and look inward. Visualize the types of people you want around you. Get very descriptive in your visualization of these particular people by fantasizing about who they would be, what incredible character traits they would have, and how they would see the world. What is their level of energy? Are they committed to living a fun-filled, exciting, and enriched life? What would they do for a living? Where would they live? How have they lived their lives? What activities would they be involved with? What kind of people would they associate with? What impact would they have on your life? What impact would you have on theirs?

Practice "in-visioning" regularly. It has worked wonders in my clients' lives—and in my own. It can do the same for you. Bringing terrific people to mind can bring them to you in body!

WHERE DO YOU FIND TERRIFIC PEOPLE?

Loneliness and unhappiness may be "blessings in disguise." The lonelier you are, the more unfulfilled you are and the more unhappy you are about the people in your life who disappoint you constantly, the more ready and the more motivated you become to get out and meet some terrific people.

After reading this chapter you now know how to identify who is terrific for you. Now you may ask, "Where do I find them?" The answer is simple. You find them everywhere! If you can't seem to find them, then you haven't looked hard enough. Besides meeting terrific people through other terrific people, as described earlier, there are a multitude of ways and places to meet them. Here is a list of twenty-five places or activities to give you some ideas of where to begin:

1. Taking a brisk walk.

2. During your daily routine.

3. Doing errands.

4. Walking a dog.

5. Waiting in line at the movies or theater.

6. Waiting for a bus, plane, train, or other transportation.

7. Working out at the gym.

8. Participating in a sport.

9. Attending a sporting event.

10. In your, their, or other people's offices.

11. At a business meeting.

12. At a doctor's appointment.

13. At a health spa.

14. At a coffee shop or restaurant.

15. In a house of worship.

16. At a seminar or lecture.

17. At any party or social event.

18. At reunions.

19. While shopping.

20. Getting your car, video, computer, or any other appliance repaired.

21. At a music or video store.

22. At a library or museum.

23. At a political activity or function.

24. In an elevator.

25. At any life-turning event: christenings, circumscisions, birthday parties, bar mitzvahs, quincenieras, sweet sixteens, weddings, anniversaries, roasts, and even funerals.

.   .   .

YOU MAY HAVE ideas of your own. The key is not to be afraid to explore them. Get creative and remember that it is up to you to make that first move and to initiate contact. Otherwise, how will you find out if they really are terrific people?

Chapter 3

Twenty Traits and Types of Terrific People

- 1. *The Feel Gooders*
- 2. *The You, You, and You Anti-Narcissists*
- 3. *The Generous Givers*
- 4. *The Non-Judgers*
- 5. *The Good Mouthers*
- 6. *The Self-Respecters*
- 7. *The Class Acts*
- 8. *The Honest Abes*
- 9. *The Lightened-Ups*
- 10. *The Cheerleaders*
- 11. *The Completely Conscious*
- 12. *The Keep-On-Goers*
- 13. *The Emotionators*
- 14. *The Win-Winners*
- 15. *The Loyalists*
- 16. *The Immediate Doers*
- 17. *The Calculated-Risk Takers*
- 18. *The Non-Victims*
- 19. *The Life Livers*
- 20. *The Enlisters*

- *Positive Mood Contagions*
- *Terrific People as Good-Luck Charms*

*A*lthough there are numerous adjectives that describe terrific people, as we saw in the last chapter, there are primarily twenty types of terrific people. Look for these qualities when seeking new friends; they are shared by most terrific people. They include the following: feel gooders, anti-Narcissists, generous givers, non-Judgers, good mouthers, self-respecters, class acts, honest people, those who don't take themselves too seriously, cheerleaders, those who are completely conscious of what is going on around them, those who recover from rejection and keep on going, those in touch with their emotions, winners, people who are loyal, those who are immediate doers, people who take calculated risks, people who refuse to be victims, those who live life to the fullest, and those who enlist others to help them and then reward them.

1. THE FEEL-GOODERS

Terrific people always bring out the best in others.
They make them feel good and as though they matter,
through their caring and kind words.

Why did the head of a Fortune 500 company, a senator, a major film star, a major rock star, a busboy, a car attendant, and a janitor think the world of Charlie Minor? Why did people gravitate toward him and want to be around him? Aside from having an upbeat and lively character, Charlie brought out the best in everyone he ever met.

He never talked down to anyone and gave everyone that

personal special touch—the acknowledgment that made people he met know he thought they were special and important.

A pharmacist I know is keenly aware of the value in treating people with respect, and thereby brings out the best in them. It helps his own economic survival as well. In an era where huge impersonal discount drugstore chains have sprung up on nearly every other block in the city, people still flock to Alan Schwab's pharmacy on Bedford Drive in Beverly Hills. The reason: Alan makes everyone who walks into his pharmacy feel like a human being. He makes them feel as though they matter. He sympathizes with their health problems and empathizes with them about their ailments. He gives them that extra personalized attention, which shows that he cares about their health and about them as human beings. As a result, Alan has many loyal customers, and his business continues to flourish. His customers feel that saving a few extra cents won't make them feel as good about themselves as going to Schwab's pharmacy, talking with Alan, and hearing him say the right words to comfort them.

Like Charlie Minor and Alan Schwab, terrific people have the ability to make others feel important. They understand what William James observed when he wrote: ''The deepest principle in human nature is the craving to be appreciated.'' They have the ability to let people know how much they are truly appreciated for their special and unique qualities.

Feel-Gooders are terrific people because they never put others down. They accept people wholeheartedly and, in so doing, bring out the best in others. This translates into their being very popular. Because they make people feel good about themselves, people want to be around them all the time.

2. THE YOU, YOU, AND YOU
ANTI-NARCISSISTS

.... ❧ ....

Terrific people are more concerned about being
"interested" than being "interesting."

"You" people are "outer" and "other" directed, meaning
that they are more concerned about the other person they are
speaking to than about themselves. Because they are interested
in finding out about you, they are less interested in trying to
entertain you. They ask a lot of questions in their attempts to
know you better and find out what you are doing, what you
are thinking, and what you are feeling; which, in turn, makes
you respond to them most favorably.

Because their universe is wide and they are interested in a
variety of things, events, people, and issues, they have many
topics to discuss besides themselves. This, in turn, makes them
more appealing and more "interesting" to others. Terrific people like these teach us that you don't have to try to be interesting—you just are when you are not focused solely on
yourself.

Anti-Narcissists are very interested in the outside world and
your part in it. Their main concern is how others think and
feel, which makes them more conscious of other people's feelings and less likely to stick their feet in their mouths. They are
always listening for certain emotional cues in the person's tone
or watching for certain revealing signs in their body language
and facial reactions. This is the main reason why most people
come away from a conversation with an Anti-Narcissist feeling
as though they were really understood. They are thrilled that
a person finally got what they were trying to say, and what
they were all about.

Anti-Narcissists are also complimentary and never judgmental. They use the "I" word only when they are relating to
what you are saying, and whatever they say will always relate
back to you. For example, if you mentioned that you played
tennis this morning, Anti-Narcissists are likely to reply that

they like to play tennis at such-and-such a club, and then to suggest that you play there together sometime. "I-I-I" or "Me-Me-Me" are not a part of their repertoire.

Mark and Ken were having a conversation about marriage in general. Suddenly Ken noticed that during certain times in the conversation, Mark squinted and frowned. Because he was interested in Mark as a person, Ken noticed that Mark's unhappy facial expressions appeared whenever Mark made a comment about his wife. Finally Mark admitted that he was having marital problems. Because of Ken's compassion, his relating his own past marital experiences and problems only as they related to Mark's specific issues, and by paying attention to Mark's verbal and nonverbal reactions, Mark became even more open to sharing his problems with Ken in even greater detail and ultimately asked Ken if he could recommend a good therapist that he and his wife could see for marital counseling.

You-You-and-You Anti-Narcissists are terrific people because of their total lack of self-involvement and self-absorption. These terrific people are never consumed with themselves. They never bore you with the details of their lives. Rather, they aim the spotlight of attention at you. Because of their interest in you, you can't help becoming interested in them, which allows for a reciprocity in the relationship and a stronger friendship.

3. THE GENEROUS GIVERS

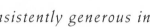

*Terrific people are consistently generous in actions
and words and are always willing to go out of
their way to help others.*

Recently I ran across the following headline in the *New York Post:* "Doc Will Aid Slashed Teen." As I read the article about a seventeen-year-old beauty queen and model whose face was slashed by a racist while she was waiting for a bus, my eyes welled up with tears. Apparently, the forty stitches that Gia

Grante, Miss Junior Teen New York, received to close her facial wounds left wide scars all over her face. When I read further, I discovered that the Manhattan plastic surgeon who offered to remove her scars for free was none other than my good friend and colleague, Dr. Robert Vitolo, with whom I share an office in Manhattan. I was even more touched, although it didn't surprise me, because Dr. Vitolo is a very generous and giving human being who always goes out of his way to help people. He helps people far beyond what surgical duties necessitate. For example, one of his clients was frustrated that she couldn't get work as a model. So he introduced her to a top modeling agent he knew, and now this young woman works all the time. These are just two examples of the wonderful, unselfish things he does for people on a daily basis—without the expectation of getting anything in return but harmony and goodwill.

Terrific people will not just do things for others if it fits into their schedule, or only if it is convenient for them. Instead, they will make the time and will go out of their way to help another person.

When Jean found out that Jonathan had broken his leg, she offered to do his grocery shopping. It wasn't a simple task of just picking up a few extra things the next time she went shopping for herself. Instead, she traveled to a neighboring city to get Jonathan the special health foods he usually ate. She took the time and effort to do what she knew Jonathan would really value and appreciate.

In the words of the great playwright Henrik Ibsen, ''A thousand words will not leave so deep an impression as one deed.'' In addition to their deeds, terrific people are generous in their words. They are generous with compliments, giving praise and recognition where due. They are free to give compliments to people they may not even know.

Claudia and her friend Michelle were walking their dogs when a handsome couple in evening dress crossed the street. Seeing them approach, Michelle whispered that they looked great. As they approached, Michelle clammed up and glanced the other way, while Claudia looked directly at the couple, smiled, and remarked, "Now, that is what I'd call a great-looking couple." The couple thanked her, chuckled, and even nuzzled closer together. Her sincere compliment and acknowledgment not only made them feel great, but reinforced them as a couple.

Generous Givers are terrific people because they are unselfish and go out of their way to be kind, to be of service, and to be helpful—expecting little or nothing in return. They do not necessarily know that they are adding good to the world.

4. THE NON-JUDGERS

Terrific people are open-minded and flexible.

Terrific people are always open to new people and new ideas. They are willing to try new things. They don't judge people based on any prejudices or preconceived notions about them. They are willing to give people the benefit of the doubt.

Even if they have heard negative things about a person, they are not willing to go by that alone. Instead, they form their own opinions.

Daphne came from a very sheltered background; she was raised to keep people "unlike" her out of her life. Her family permitted her to associate with and to date only people of her own ethnic background and religious sect. Because Daphne was a National Merit Scholarship winner, she was recruited by some of the major universities in the country. Even though her parents struggled with her going away from home, she fought with them until they relented. Even though they couldn't pass up the offer of free tuition, they wrestled with the fear that she would be among "other kinds" of people—ones who might influence her and turn her away from her religion and her traditions. Their fears were correct. Four years later, Daphne emerged from college an entirely different person—

a terrific person devoid of the ugly prejudices her parents had forced upon her in their ignorance. She realized that it didn't matter what religion, skin color, or ethnic origin a person had. She concluded that it was stupid and ridiculous to keep someone out of her life just because some of her ancestors had fought against some of these groups generations earlier. She figured out that it was the ignorance and stupidity of closing "others" out by thinking that their way was the only right way to live or to pray that created so much hatred in the world. Because of the extremely toxic reaction of Daphne's father to her new views (which nearly led to violence against her), Daphne left home for good and made a life for herself traveling around the world and filling and enriching her life with people from all different ethnic backgrounds.

Terrific people don't judge others based on their lifestyles. They sincerely believe that if it makes the other person happy, then so be it—as long as it doesn't harm anyone. Just as terrific people don't judge people based on their ethnic origins, they refrain similarly from making judgments about people based on their sexual preferences.

Sabina Basch, owner of A Plus Models, one of the most popular modeling agencies in New York, told me that starting her agency has been the biggest gift in her life. It taught her the valuable lesson of never judging a person. Before she started her agency, she admitted that in the past, like many others, she harbored some extreme prejudices against "strange-looking people." In fact, she couldn't understand how someone could actually be a drag queen. She wondered how a man would ever want to put on makeup—let alone a dress—until she met enough drag queens through her work and realized quickly that they were just like everyone else, complete with feelings, emotions, and sensitivities. She acknowledged that she also had judgmental feelings about obese people until she met enough people who liked who they were and how they looked, despite society's value system. A Plus Models now represents everyone from infants to drag queens, tattooed to pierced people, from short people to high-fashion models, to teens, to the physically and mentally challenged. Running the agency has opened up a whole new world to Sabina, who shares her open-minded views about loving and not judging people regularly in the many television appearances she makes each year.

Non-Judgers are terrific people because they accept themselves and others. In addition, flexibility with their views and open-mindedness to new people, ideas, and experiences enables them to be flexible about how they lead their lives.

5. THE GOOD MOUTHERS

Terrific people never bad-mouth others.

Paul Bloch, cochairman of the board of Rogers and Cowan Inc., has been one of Hollywood's top publicists for the past twenty-five years. He has worked with such stars as Sylvester Stallone, Bruce Willis, and John Travolta. One of the reasons why everyone respects and trusts Paul Bloch (in an industry that all too often thrives on malicious gossip and bad-mouthing others) is because he never says a bad word about anyone, at any time, under any circumstances. In a room full of people gossiping about a "toxic" person, Paul will say nothing negative. It doesn't matter what the person did. He or she could be a terror of a client, extremely difficult and poisonous to deal with, but Paul will always maintain his philosophy, which he told me was ingrained in him as a child by his late mother: "If you can't say anything nice about someone, don't say anything at all." Even though many of us have heard this mantra while growing up, the terrific people abide by it. If they feel that the person is horrible or "toxic," they won't discuss it in public.

Good Mouthers usually spend their time singing the praises of others. They will tell practically everyone they know, and new people they meet, about the "terrific special friends" they have, building them up every chance they get. Good Mouthers are terrific because they have a genuine affection for people. They are so conscious about hurting others that they never want to contribute to sullying the reputation of anyone else. Good Mouthers are also terrific because since they are usually focusing on the good traits of others, they don't spend much time paying attention to their negative traits.

6. THE SELF-RESPECTERS

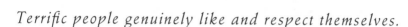

Terrific people genuinely like and respect themselves.

Nobody can tell terrific people something negative about themselves because they just won't buy it. Because they like and respect themselves, they have an abundance of self-confidence, which spills over to other people. Since they will never allow themselves to be treated with anything less than respect and dignity, they are never victims or masochists. If someone doesn't treat them in a manner they believe they should be treated, that person will definitely know about it and/or will no longer be part of their lives. Terrific people are usually so kind and gracious and respectful to others because they tend to treat others how they wish to be treated.

So it was no surprise when Christina refused to be treated in a sarcastic manner. Since she would never think of treating anyone else that way, it wasn't how she expected to be treated. When Gray made an unwarranted, sarcastic comment to her, she called him on it immediately, which made him fumble and mumble a lame excuse and an eventual apology.

Self-Respecters are terrific people because they genuinely like themselves, they are usually warm, friendly, and outgoing. You can often see them walking down the street with a big smile on their face, looking at others and saying hello even to strangers as they pass by them. Being alert to the existence of others, they always seem to be upbeat and in a good mood because their abundance of good feelings about themselves translates into good feeling and goodwill toward others.

7. THE CLASS ACTS

Terrific people remember the little things that count when it comes to relationships.

Debbie suffered a miscarriage and was devastated. Melinda knew that there was nothing she could do to alleviate her dear friend Debbie's pain, but she made herself available to Debbie twenty-four hours a day. She encouraged Debbie to call her whenever she felt down and not to worry about disturbing or imposing on her. Melinda sent over a masseuse for daily massages, as she knew how comforting that would be. She sent over a maid who also prepared meals twice a week, and paid for it, so that Debbie would be less stressed. She encouraged Debbie to talk to a therapist who could be even more helpful. Melinda paid attention to the details of Debbie's life so that she could not only be there to comfort her, but to alleviate her stress. Debbie has so much love and appreciation for Melinda. Because of her attention to the things that rarely anybody ever thinks of or does, their friendship took on a new dimension. She saw what a true friend Melinda was and how much she really cared.

Terrific people often go out of their way to remember the small details: a person's favorite color, birthday, or likes or dislikes. Even though the late film director Louis Malle was dying of cancer, he took the time to pay attention to the small details before his passing. He remembered that his lovely wife, actress Candice Bergen, admired a certain bracelet once while they were shopping together. On his deathbed, he called the jewelers and purchased the bracelet. He instructed that it be sent to his wife on her birthday, after his death, revealing what a truly terrific person he was.

Class Act people not only consistently remember the details of what makes you happy. In doing so, they show you that they acknowledge you and want to please you. For example, Don knew that Marlene collected teapots and that her favorite color was yellow, so he took the time to seek out a bright yellow teapot as a gift—for no special reason other than to let her know that he liked her and that she was important to him. This gesture endeared Don to Marlene and was the turning point in cementing their relationship.

Class Act people are terrific because their goals in relationships are to please and delight others. They are consistent esteem builders: highly generous, creative, and innovative. They appreciate the finer things in life as they share ways to make other lives a lot easier—and a lot richer in quality.

8. THE HONEST ABES

Terrific people are honest and straightforward.

Some of the most terrific businesspeople in the world have been around the longest because they have treated people honestly and fairly. Many of the great motivators—from Dr. Norman Vincent Peale to Zig Ziglar—realize the importance of honesty and integrity. They share the belief: "All a person has is his or her word."

Terrific people keep their word. When they say they are going to do something, they do it! You can always count on them to show up when they are expected to, to meet a deadline on time, and to tell you what is really going on. They don't speak in double messages. They speak the truth at all times. If they can't do something that they promised to do, or if plans fall through, they will not make up phony excuses. Instead, they will tell you the truth.

Terrific people are not phony, bullshitters, or manipulators.

They are straightforward and forthright, and always try to say and do the right thing.

Academy Award–winning film producer Arnold Kopelson, who has produced such memorable films as *Platoon, The Fugitive, Outbreak, Seven, Eraser,* and *Mad City,* is one of the few heavyweights in the Hollywood motion-picture industry whom almost everyone loves and respects. Directors, actors, studios, and investors are all anxious to do business with him because he is honest and dependable. When he says that he will bring a film in within a certain time, or at a certain budget, he does just that. When he promises people that he will help them, he follows through. In a business that is based on illusion, slick talking, and hype, Arnold Kopelson is a rare gem. Everyone who comes in contact with him recognizes this fact and appreciates his honesty, fairness, and respectful treatment of people.

Others are eager to do business and associate with the Honest Abe because they feel that they can trust him or her. This trust allows people to feel more secure with the way business will be conducted (in an up-front aboveboard manner) and further alleviates additional tensions caused by making sure that the person isn't taking advantage or cheating you.

9. THE LIGHTENED-UPS

Terrific people never take themselves too seriously.

Terrific people can make fun of themselves, which makes them all the more endearing to others. They also never pontificate inappropriately, going on and on about their views on serious matters when they are losing their audience or people aren't relating to them. They know when to lighten up, let go of all tension, and not get bent out of shape if things don't go exactly their way. They use humor, laughter, or a lighthearted attitude to help them to roll with the punches. This attitude explains why their faces are usually open and there is little muscle tension (reflecting anger) in the corners of their mouths and lips. As a result, people are more drawn to them because they find them to be more approachable.

Lightened-Up people are terrific because their lack of up-tightness and nervousness makes others feel more comfortable around them. People tend to be drawn to them and find their lightheartedness to be contagious.

10. THE CHEERLEADERS

Terrific people are your main supporters—and your cheerleaders.

Because they are not jealous and envious of others, terrific people are extremely supportive of others. They encourage others and want the best for them, so they consistently encourage them to feel good about themselves, especially when those others are in doubt of themselves or their abilities. Cheerleaders won't tolerate others engaging in negative self-talk. Instead, they work to bring out the best in people.

Carrie was a concert pianist who was constantly putting herself down. Nothing escaped her criticism—from her looks to her abilities. She was a beautiful woman and extraordinarily talented. Whenever she tore herself down, her terrific friend Rosalyn would not tolerate it. She would buoy her up repeatedly, telling her how great she was. Rosalyn never got tired of building up Carrie's ego and self-esteem because she knew that Carrie needed to have the truth of her greatness reflected back at her. With Rosalyn influencing her life positively, Carrie developed more and more self-confidence and found herself believing in her own abilities and unique qualities a lot more, which allowed her to perform much better (according to her) and to seek out other performance opportunities.

Terrific people act as cheerleaders for others by singing their praises to as many people as they can. They network for you.

They help you build your business because they believe in you. They are always keeping you in mind with whomever they meet. Vanessa, one of my former terrific clients whom I treated ten years ago, has sent me numerous clients throughout the years. Because she felt that our work together was instrumental in changing the quality of her life, she told me that she never forgot our sessions and the valuable things she learned while working with me. As a result of her satisfaction, she wanted people whom she knew to have the same positive experience she did. Therefore, throughout the years, Vanessa has referred countless clients as she continues to sing my praises, for which I am wholeheartedly appreciative.

Cheerleaders are terrific people because their energy tends to bring you more energy. Because Cheerleaders are 100 percent behind you and are so supportive, they tend to motivate you to be your very best. Because they appreciate who you are, they reflect your finest qualities back to you and thereby allow you to appreciate yourself a lot more.

11. THE COMPLETELY CONSCIOUS

Terrific people think of other people's feelings first and know exactly what to say in good times and in bad.

Completely Conscious people are always totally aware of their surroundings and of what is going on around them. This quality means not only that they seldom have accidents or rarely become victims of crime, but also that they are always on the alert for the verbal and nonverbal communication of other people. The Completely Conscious rarely put their "foot in their mouth," commit faux pas, or say mean or inappropriate things to others accidentally. They know when to speak and when to be silent.

Like Antinarcissists, they are observant of manners, proper

etiquette and, most importantly, the feelings of others. They are aware of others' mental and emotional states, and what crises they may be going through. The Completely Conscious live by the Golden Rule. They always do unto others as they would have others do unto them. They are considerate, consistent, and generous. Because of their heightened level of awareness, they find it easy to remember people's faces and names as well as topics from previous conversations. They are genuinely supportive. If they need to instruct or give advice, they will often couch what they are about to say with phrases and statements like "Let me know if you would like my opinion," or "May I give you some advice?" Whenever they do give advice, they do so lovingly and supportively. Depending on the person's response, they act accordingly, respecting the other person's feelings at all times.

Gus knew that his brother George was making a huge mistake by marrying Ariana, whom everyone suspected was a gold digger. He also knew that he couldn't even attempt to convince his brother differently because George had made up his mind to marry Ariana. Being Completely Conscious of George's stand on the issue, Gus said, "You know, George, if anyone came up to me before my wedding and told me not to marry the woman I was going to marry, I would punch him right in the face. So, brother, I'm giving you the opportunity to do just that. Go ahead, hit me."

They both started to laugh, and Gus was able to break through the ice. Suddenly the tension left George's body and the two brothers hugged each other. With his arm still around George, Gus said, "You know I love you not because you're my brother, but because of who you turned out to be, a decent man whom I respect and look up to. All I want to do is to see you happy. But, my brother, you haven't been very happy with Ariana since you first started dating two years ago."

Suddenly Gus noticed George's eyes widen as his eyebrows rose, indicating that there was some truth in what Gus had to say. Observing his brother's physical reaction, Gus continued by saying, "Look, you have been unfaithful to Ariana throughout your dating, and you have to ask yourself why you have had to look at other women when supposedly you are in love with her. You yell at her constantly and she yells at you. This isn't the way things are supposed to be. In fact, there were times when I thought you two would kill each other. All you do is fight about stupid, petty things. So why do you want to marry someone and to spend the rest of your life fighting with her instead of loving and respecting her?''

George responded in a harsh, loud voice. ''Gus, I don't really want to marry her. I felt pressured. She gave me an ultimatum. If I didn't marry her, she said I couldn't see her again. Now that all the families know, and she has her dress and all, I have to go through with it.''

They both looked at each other. George's eyes welled up with tears as George said, ''Go with your feelings and trust them. You are sharp enough to know that you can't live the rest of your life fighting and in constant emotional pain because a woman has already bought a dress.''

They hugged each another, and then George began to sob. The tears turned to laughter as George realized what his brother had said. There was a sigh of relief as George knew that his instincts and his brother's words rang true. Relieved, he broke off the wedding.

Because Gus was so Completely Conscious of George's feelings, he was able to reach into his brother's psyche and communicate with him on a level that was not antagonistic, and therefore he could reflect what his brother was truly feeling about the situation. He did so by being aware of his brother's actions and reactions constantly throughout their conversation and throughout their relationship.

12. THE KEEP-ON-GOERS

Terrific people recover from rejection more quickly and keep on going.

Everyone hates to be rejected or to feel unwelcome. Keep-on-Goers may feel the hurt and pain—perhaps even more intensely and deeply than others. What makes them different is that after a short period of time, they are able to let go of the pain and the hurt and move on. They don't wallow in a tub of pain feeling sorry for themselves. They start thinking about what to do next.

They jump out of the self-pity hole and move into action. They use the rejection as a motivator and as a learning tool to examine their own behaviors and discover what they may have done to contribute to the rejection.

Most successful people have had to deal with a lot of rejection, because they take more risks than most people. Some of the most famous success stories that you read about in the newspapers and magazines are of people who have suffered the pain of rejection. My client Michael, one of the richest and most successful men in this country, has made millions and also lost millions. He has been accepted by many and rejected by even more. He told me that the only thing that was constant while he was being rejected was that he kept getting up whenever he was knocked down. He never retreated and never lost his ambition or sight of his goal, just because others didn't see his point of view. He just tried new and innovative ways to make it, and certainly did—right to the top. Madonna, Oprah Winfrey, Dustin Hoffman, Sylvester Stallone, and Melanie Griffith all experienced the excruciating pain of rejection. They didn't listen to the naysayers, those who didn't believe in them or people who were downright mean and obnoxious to them. They dealt with their pain and kept moving ahead until they became not only stars, but superstars.

Keep-on-Goers are terrific people because they inspire others. They have so much conviction and belief in themselves that they don't dwell on the rejection, but instead focus on accomplishing their goals. They act as an inspiration to us all, emphasizing the need to continue on in the face of adversity.

13. THE EMOTIONATORS

Terrific people allow themselves to be uninhibited, open, and vulnerable.

Emotionators aren't afraid to let others know they are human, that they are scared, nervous, or unsure. They never try to keep that stiff upper lip or to keep up a brave front. Instead, when they experience an emotion, they aren't afraid to show it.

Emotionators aren't afraid to feel pain, sadness, or joy. They aren't inhibited in their expression of emotion, whether they are feeling anger, fear, surprise, doubt, compassion, or love. They are able to express themselves physically, through their body and facial actions, as well as vocally, in the tones of their voices.

Steve Allen is a public-relations consultant who is the ultimate Emotionator. His infectious, upbeat emotional tone, on the phone and in person, has made his business the success that it is today. Whenever Steve calls on the media, they are eager to hear what he has to say because his message comes across clearly and enthusiastically. If he is genuinely excited about a client, his confidence in his client is reflected through his vocal tone, which usually translates into the client's getting booked as a guest on the television show for which he is pitching them.

Emotionators are a terrific people because they are able to fine-tune their communications with others. Not only are they aware of their own emotions, but they are equally aware of the emotions of others. This makes them both more receptive and more responsive to the emotional states of others. They are also excellent empathizers. When someone is telling them about a sad situation, they not only feel the emotion, but are able to show their feelings toward the other person. Because Emotionators are more in tune with other people's feelings, those around them tend to feel more open and emotionally safe and secure.

14. THE WIN-WINNERS

Terrific people are win-win oriented.

Win-Winners are not happy to see that they have won while others have lost. Instead, they want to see that both sides have won. Both in their business and in their personal lives, they want everyone to come out of a situation feeling good. They are not willing only to take, but to give as well. They don't want to see others unhappy, disappointed, or with hurt feelings. As a result, they are excellent negotiators.

People like doing business with Jason because, in every negotiation, he wants everyone to walk away feeling that they got something out of the deal. In his transactions with people, he never negotiates for the last nickel and dime. Instead he is more concerned with the big picture. He has learned that having his customers walk away happy is worth so much more in the long run than the minor costs he incurs in doing so. Because they feel he is fair with them, they do repeat business with him. In addition, his customer base has grown exponentially because most of the people he does business with send their friends and relatives over to Jason.

Win-Winners are terrific people because they are usually fair, forthright, and open-minded. They look at issues from the viewpoint of the other party, not just their own. As a result, they are not selfish. They want the best for everyone concerned.

15. THE LOYALISTS

Terrific people are loyal and compassionate.

Loyalists do not change with every wind. They are not wishy-washy kiss-up people. Instead, they are committed to their beliefs and are consistent with the people with whom they associate. These individuals have no difficulty making a decision and sticking to it. They are fearless and are not held back by what others may think of them. They are confident: they know who they are, know what they think is right, and know how to behave in almost all situations.

Dave was at a social gathering when he overheard three men tearing down his colleague Norm. He was certainly aware that Norm had some problems and wasn't perfect, but he wasn't going to stand there and not defend his colleague's honor. He walked over to the three men casually and told them politely that he couldn't help overhearing their conversation about Norm. And although he could see their point of view, he wanted to add another perspective to the situation. The three men listened carefully and suddenly their tight and angry faces softened. Their loud, harsh tones became softer and gentler. Now they had another viewpoint, and with that understood clearly why Norm behaved the way he did.

It took a lot of guts for Dave to walk over to the three men in the first place, but what took even more guts was defending his friend when the majority of people around were vehemently against him.

Loyalists are terrific people because they know the meaning of commitment. They are not afraid to speak up on behalf of someone or something in which they believe. Most people admire them because they have guts and backbone. If there is a problem, Loyalists will confront the situation head-on. Therefore, you always know where you stand with them. You will always know what decisions they made as soon as possible; they will never leave you wondering or hanging in limbo.

16. THE IMMEDIATE DOERS

Immediate Doers earn a lot of respect from others because they are responsible, get things done immediately, and respect other people's time.

When Immediate Doers promise something, they follow through immediately. They never procrastinate. Their word is their bond. You can always depend on the Immediate Doer. When they say something will be delivered at six o' clock, it is there at six on the dot. When they say that they will show up at a party, they will be there. Not only do they keep their obligations but they also believe that doing things *now* ensures that they will get done. Some of the most successful people I have worked with were Immediate Doers. There is a saying, "If you want to get something done, give it to the busiest person." This is true because the busiest people don't have any time to waste. They do things as soon as they are asked. You never have to ask twice. Asking once is as good as knowing that the job is done. If they are too busy, or overwhelmed by a project deadline, they will often enlist the help of an assistant or a friend to make sure the job is done.

When you ask them to fax or to send something, they won't let it sit in a pile and then get to it two weeks later. Instead, they do things immediately.

One of the reasons why I work so well with my assistant is that we are both Immediate Doers. I respect her time constraints and she respects mine. As a result, we are able to work efficiently and smoothly in getting things done in a limited amount of time. Immediate Doers are terrific people because they are accountable, responsible, and never disappoint people or create additional stress and frustration for others by putting off or violating their commitments. They also respect others and pay close attention to their needs. The immediacy with which they do things for you most often reflects their respect for you. If, by some chance, they cannot meet a deadline or get something done immediately, out of respect, they will let you know exactly when they can do it.

17. THE CALCULATED-RISK TAKERS

Terrific people are not afraid to jump in and take calculated risks in order to pursue their dreams.

Because terrific people seek growth, they are not afraid to do whatever it takes to contribute to their personal growth process. Terrific people can afford to take more calculated risks because they trust their guts. They know themselves so well and believe in themselves so strongly that they go with their instincts, and usually discover that they have done the right thing.

Ron had a very successful medical practice in a small town, a beautiful home, many material things, and wonderful toys. But none of this meant anything to him. He worked day and night and never had any time for himself. At the age of forty, he woke up one morning to find that even though he seemingly had it all, he felt that he had nothing. He wasn't happy. He was overworked and exhausted most of the time. The little free time he did have was devoted to errands, getting organized, and repairing things around the house. As far as he was concerned, he had no life, and he wanted to change that situation. His first step was to figure out how much money he had in the bank. Then he put his home, cars, motorcycle, and other toys up for sale, and moved to Los Angeles to become a stand-up comedian. He took a calculated risk, figuring that he had enough to live on for several years without working. If he had to work, he knew that he could get his California medical license and work in an emergency room part-time. Or he could get a job on film sets, since the industry usually hires medical personnel when films go on location.

Even though Ron took a risk in letting go of his practice,

deep inside he knew he would be all right and would not starve as he sought his dream.

Shortly after arriving in Los Angeles, opportunity knocked, and Ron performed at an amateur night at a comedy club. He has been traveling across the country ever since, performing at many comedy clubs. Even though he makes a pittance of what he earned as a physician, he has never been happier in his life.

Calculated-Risk Takers are terrific people because they figure out how they can live out their dreams intelligently and systematically. They are not afraid to try new things and take chances. They decide what they need to do and they go ahead and do it, knowing they have options along the way. Calculated-Risk Takers inspire those around them who always wanted to do something different with their lives, but were afraid to take a risk.

18. THE NON-VICTIMS

Terrific people know their strengths and weaknesses and take full responsibility for their actions.

Non-Victims are realists. They are sure of themselves. They know their good points and bad points, strong and weak points. They take full responsibility for their lots in life, and know that they are responsible for their own happiness or unhappiness. They are not afraid to get out of toxic situations that no longer work for them. They do not wallow in self-pity.

Tom was working for a company for ten years when there was a change in his department and he got a new boss. This man was an insecure control freak and a bully who tried to make Tom's life a living hell. After a week of this, Tom saw the writing on the wall. Because he didn't want to lose his benefits with the company, he immediately looked for and took another position within the company. He didn't care that it was a lateral move; anything was better than being around his new boss. Tom saw the problem right away, took responsibility for his own feelings of unhappiness at work, and did something about it immediately—he changed departments.

Dara was dating Guy for a year. They loved each other. But Guy didn't want to get married. He had gone through a messy divorce two years earlier, had three young children, and didn't want to have any more kids. He had mountains of alimony and child-support bills. After he explained this to Dara, she made the conscious decision to get off his case and stop bugging him about marrying her. She loved him. He loved her. They had a great time and very little tension between them, so there was no problem except for a piece of paper. By letting go of her unhappiness about not being married, and letting in the love Guy gave consistently, Dara no longer had a problem. She made a conscious adult decision to stay with Guy, and she has not regretted it.

Non-Victims are terrific people because they take full responsibility for their lives and don't blame others for their unhappiness. If they feel unhappy about a situation, they know that it is up to them to handle it and to try to change it. They know that it is completely up to them. They are adults and act like adults in their decision making. They are not self-pitying and don't burden others with their troubles. They do, however, let other helpful terrific people into their lives, and they don't shun others who try to give them helpful and supportive advice.

19. THE LIFE LIVERS

*Terrific people never rest on their laurels. They
continue to seek out their passions*

Life Livers don't live in the past. Whether they have done
good or bad things, they move ahead because they are growers.
They live in the present and are future driven. They get into
everything they do with passion and zest. They love life and
live it to the fullest. Like the Calculated-Risk Takers, Non-
Victims, Immediate Doers, Keep-on-Goers, and Self-
Respecters, they go after their dreams. They reach out with
both hands and grasp what life has to offer. Fred Dalton
Thompson is a Life Liver whom I truly respect and admire.
He never rested on his laurels, and he had much to rest on.
After graduating at the top of his law-school class at Vanderbilt
University, he went on to become the youngest Watergate
prosecutor and one of the country's most successful attorneys.
He had offices in Nashville, New York, and Washington, D.C.
With all that, he didn't rest on his successes and he entered a
new arena—as an actor in Hollywood. He went on to become
one of the most sought-after performers in Hollywood, ap-
pearing in many box-office hits, from *The Hunt for Red October*
to *In the Line of Fire*. Once again, he didn't rest on his accomplishments, but still kept moving ahead and is now a United
States senator from the state of Tennessee.

Just as terrific people bounce back quickly from rejection,
they bounce back quickly from success as well. Although they
are proud of themselves and their accomplishments, they use
these accomplishments as building blocks to the next level of
their lives and their development. They continue to grow by
moving ahead, accomplishing more and more, and giving all
that they have to offer. Like Non-Judgers, Life Livers are also
willing to go with the flow. They aren't neurotic and rigid;
things don't have to go completely as planned, or "their way
or forget it," for them to be happy. Whenever they get
stressed out about something or other not working out, they

remind themselves to go with the tide: There are certain things they can change and certain things they can't. They do not become overwhelmed by what they can't change.

Life Livers are such terrific people because they experience so much joy from life that their attitudes can often be contagious. They are exciting to talk to and exciting to be around. Their minds are always working, and they are always ready for some new action and new adventure. They never sit still and worry about their woes because they are too busy living—and contributing excitement, joy, and beauty to their own and others' lives.

20. THE ENLISTERS

Terrific people enroll people who can help them reach their goals—and reward them accordingly.

Enlisters realize that they need other people to help them achieve their goals, so they try to enroll others who believe in them and in their aims. They are credible, sincere, and passionate about their goals and beliefs.

Like the Three Musketeers, their philosophy is "All for one and one for all." Although they take advantage of every opportunity that comes their way, they do not use people because they are not selfish and manipulative, nor are they unappreciative of others' efforts. Similar to the Win-Winner, they want everyone to come out ahead and to benefit from any given situation.

Enlisters try to get people to help them by encouraging them to understand and appreciate their aims. If the people they have enlisted don't follow through or turn out to be flaky or unsupportive, they cut their losses immediately and look elsewhere. They move on and try to find other people who share the same beliefs in them, and goals. Similar to the Keep-on-Goer, Enlisters don't sit and dwell on why someone did them wrong, wasn't on their side, or rejected them. Because they have Non-victim traits, they move on quickly and painlessly.

Acting is perhaps the most difficult profession of all. It is not that acting is so difficult, but that finding the right people who believe in you—a team 100 percent on your side, who believes in you over a long period of time—is excruciatingly difficult and almost nearly impossible to find.

I once knew a man who moved to California with one jacket, two shirts, a pair of jeans, and only $200 in his pocket. He lived in his car and worked three jobs to support his dream of becoming an actor. Even though he could barely make ends meet, he had an upbeat attitude and did whatever it took to hone his skills: He attended acting classes, improved his speaking voice by working with me, and joined a gym (so he could not only work out, but take a shower every day). He was able to pay for these things by doing odd jobs here and there. He was not only dedicated and hardworking, but also very likable. He always had a big smile and a kind word for everyone with whom he came in contact, no matter what problems he was facing.

I respected him so much that I introduced him to a talent agent, who took him on. Soon afterward, his acting teacher, who also liked and respected him, arranged a meeting between him and a director who was casting a film. The director hired him immediately, and because he was so pleasant to be around and so easy to work with, the director hired him for his next film, as well. As a result, his agent believed in him more and got him more auditions for more and more films. Ultimately, he became a huge star.

Why did so many people, including myself, want to do things for this man? To open doors? To help him achieve his goals? It is very simple. He was an Enlister, who knew how to attract terrific people to his life.

So is a popular actress I know and her manager.

This actress is perhaps one of the most terrific people I have ever met in my life. She has most of the twenty terrific-people traits. She is the epitome of the Enlister—you can't help wanting to do everything possible to help her. Her personal manager is just as terrific as she is. She discovered my client, and from day one believed in her talents and her goals. She supported her and encouraged her when times were tough, and is now there to reap the rewards of her efforts. The actress appreciated her manager's past support and is there supporting her manager right back.

Enlisters are terrific people because of their passion to excite, lead, and move people. In essence, they are modern-day Pied Pipers, collecting and caring for people who follow them.

Their openness and sincerity make people want to do things for them. And what makes them most special is their loyalty to others; they appreciate and reward those who are on their team. They give back what they have received—a hundredfold.

POSITIVE MOOD CONTAGIONS

Just as being around "toxic" people can put you into a bad mood, being around terrific people can put you in a great mood. This is especially true for people who are highly sensitive to others because they tend to mimic or mirror the vocal tones, body language, and facial expressions of terrific people.

When Tammy was in high school, she was unkempt, never cared about or for herself, was disorganized, always seemed to be in a bad mood, and had a bad attitude. She had few friends and average grades. However, this all changed when she went away to college and roomed with Angela. Angela was a wonderful person whose warmth and positivity had a profound effect on Tammy's attitude. Tammy looked up to Angela and always seemed to feel great whenever she was around her. Students who attended Tammy's college who knew her from high school couldn't believe it was the same person. Tammy actually smiled and said hello to others as she passed them in the corridors at the university, something she never would have dreamed of doing in high school. Tammy was more studious, helpful to others, and her tone of voice was sweeter, softer, and more mellifluous. When Tammy returned home for Christmas vacation, nobody recognized her. She was beautiful, polished, and, most important of all, she had a more positive attitude. Angela was a terrific influence on her and helped to elevate her self-esteem.

I will never forget when I was a health, psychology, and image reporter and appeared regularly on Channel 7 KABC News (the ABC affiliate in Los Angeles). I worked there several days a week, couldn't wait to show up at the station, and hated to leave because I was in the greatest mood whenever I was there. In fact, so was everyone else who worked there. It was a special time and a special place. Perhaps the key reason why this station held the number-one ratings in the country for the five years in a row that I was there was its positive atmosphere.

People sincerely adored one another, giving one another supportive hugs and kisses, dancing, laughing, and joking around before we went on the air. Everyone there respected one another and was friendly, helpful, and supportive to each other. From the security guards to the reporters, from the editors to the writers, the cameramen and sound men to the gaffers, assignment editors, news director, and general manager. It was truly the *Eyewitness News* "family."

This experience showed me the power of being around terrific people who are usually in good and positive moods and how contagious it can be to others. No matter what mood you were in when you first arrived, after a few moments, you would start to feel much better and notice that you were smiling more. When it was quitting time, you wouldn't want to leave because you were having so much fun. When you finally left, you found that you were in a happy mood that lasted a long time because their positivity rubbed off on you. There is certainly more productivity, less tension, more fun, and more feeling great about yourself when you are around people who are usually happy and in good moods.

TERRIFIC PEOPLE AS GOOD-LUCK CHARMS

When you associate with terrific people, good things will start to happen to you. I once went to a benefit honoring Bette Midler, who said that her luck changed when she married her terrific husband. She was embraced by Hollywood, made several hit films, wrote several hit songs, and became a mother to a wonderful little girl.

Several of my clients have relayed similar stories to me— they have gotten the jobs they always wanted and improved their entire lifestyles after associating with a special terrific person.

Some people believe that there is a karmic or metaphysical component to why this may happen, while others believe that because a person is happy, more positive, more relaxed, less uptight, easier to be around, he or she is therefore more receptive to life's golden opportunities.

Whatever you believe, know that with more terrific people in your life, you will indeed lead a charmed life.

Chapter 4

Finding and Attracting Terrific People to Fill Your Life

- *Forget the First Four Minutes—It's Now the First Four Seconds*
- *The Initial Attraction*
- *Attracting Terrific People with the Outer You*
- *Attracting Potential Terrific People with a Smile and a Warm Hello*
- *Attracting Terrific People by the Way You Speak—It's Not What You Say, It's How You Say It!*
- *Your Body Talks, Too!*
- *The Art of the Gesture*
- *Your Handshake Makes an Immediate Impression*
- *To Touch or Not to Touch?—That Is the Question*
- *Your Face Speaks 1000 Words*
- *It's Not Just How You Say It—It's What You Say That Counts!*
- *Shy People Are Selfish People*
- *How to Have a Great Conversation: What Do You Say After You've Said Hello?*

*I*n this chapter, you will learn how to develop your own unique interests and talents and how to improve your communication skills to help you bring more terrific people to your life.

Because communication involves much more than words, you will learn about body language (posture, gestures, facial expressions) and speech and voice production. Your body language communicates a great deal to those around you, which can greatly affect how they relate to you.

You will also learn other essential skills necessary to create a life filled with terrific people—such as eliminating toxic relationships and pettiness from your life. Once you rid your life of these negative forces, you will have much more energy for new and wonderful relationships, which will help you to fulfill your dreams—and, just as importantly, help you to help others fulfill theirs.

By learning and practicing the skills necessary for maintaining these relationships, the respect, sincerity, appreciation, warmth, kindness, and openness will come back to you a thousandfold.

FORGET THE FIRST FOUR MINUTES— IT'S NOW THE FIRST FOUR SECONDS

Over two decades ago *Contact: The First Four Minutes*, by Dr. Leonard Zunin created a great deal of controversy. Critics of the book refused to believe that you could make an accurate decision about a person in just four minutes. You need much more time than that—you need to get to know a person by spending time with him or her before you can make an accurate decision about them.

Dr. Zunin was definitely on the right track in believing that we can assess and form opinions about people in a very short period of time. Today, with our advanced satellite technology that lets us see what is actually happening around the globe in real time, we make immediate decisions about people in a matter of seconds.

Look how we feel about people we watch on television. We either like them or we can't stand them. We judge them as winners or losers, liars, or "Honest Abes." Based on a moment's glance at the television, we even place pejorative labels on them like "pervert," "jerk," or "manipulator."

We all have opinions, and we often make those opinions in seconds by watching and listening to snippets of what people say and how they comport themselves. Is it any wonder that first impressions are still so powerful and important—and can make the difference between attracting or repelling new people?

THE INITIAL ATTRACTION

We form our opinions of others based on what goes on inside us, what we feel, how their presence affects us. We are attracted to people for a multitude of reasons, most of which are personal and uniquely ingrained in our individual psyches. For example, you may be partial to tall, thin, willowy, dark-haired women because they may remind you of a baby-sitter you were attracted to when you were a young boy. This process of feeling the attraction to the familiar, the known, is called imprinting.

CARLA IS ATTRACTED only to huge football player-type men because the love of her life, whom she dated throughout her high-school years, was a huge football player. Being a large woman herself, whenever she was in his arms, she not only felt safe and secure, but also small and feminine. It brought out the best in her in terms of her sensuality and her sexuality.

Her attraction to this physical type was imprinted into her psyche early in her sexual development, and it remains today. Even though she has been intimate with other men who don't fit this type, she finds that she is most stimulated when she is with a physically larger man.

This may also explain why men, depending on their age group and the era in which they grew up, are physically attracted to certain types of women. For example, men in their fifties and sixties are often drawn to buxom, full-figured, voluptuous, women—like the ones they may have admired while growing up during their sexually formative years: women like Marilyn Monroe, Jayne Mansfield, Ava Gardner, and Jane Russell.

On the other hand, men in their late thirties and forties are often attracted attracted to thinner model-type figures because the ideal female body of their generation was characterized by Twiggy, Jean Shrimpton, and many other models. In contrast, men in their twenties and early thirties have been imprinted with the athletic, curvy-yet-muscular woman like Cindy Crawford or Naomi Campbell.

It would be too simplistic to say that all men in these generations follow types. There are too many other factors to consider. But, as a general rule, imprinting is a very powerful factor in how we come to a decision as to whom we find attractive.

To further explore the notion of what people specifically find attractive in others, I interviewed over one hundred people, both men and women, between the ages of sixteen and sixty-seven, and asked them what was the first thing that attracted them to another person. I received many answers, with eyes, body, and smile taking the top three spots, respectively. Other answers included breasts—size and shape (for men), teeth, personality, sense of humor, hair, lips, an air of self-confidence, how much money they had (women), whether they looked classy and elegant, butt, thighs, legs, their height, bone structure, intelligence, and how they smelled.

In my survey, I was surprised to discover that out of one hundred people questioned, nobody mentioned the voice or the way a person spoke, even though research shows us that the way a person speaks has an incredibly powerful impact on how we feel about them—and how we relate to them.

To further explore this impact, I conducted another study where I enrolled a beautiful woman who had a nice speaking voice to come into a room and meet several people. After she left the room, I asked both the men and women in the room what they thought of her, and how they would rate her from one to ten. While her overall score was a nine, every man in the room gave her a perfect ten. Their comments included: "she had it all," "she was not only brilliant, but gorgeous," "she was sexy," "she was breathtaking," and "she was fabulous."

Next, I escorted this same woman into a room with another group of people. But this time she spoke in a severely nasal, whiny high-pitched voice. This group rated her as being much less attractive. Now her scores ranged from as low as a two to as high as only a six, for both men and women. Some of the comments included: "she wasn't too bright," "she was a bimbo," "she was annoying," and "I couldn't stand her."

Even though we may not be conscious why we like or dislike another person, the way they speak is often the underlying reason why we react to the person as we do.

The ingredient that remains constant in terms of attracting others to you is the way in which you communicate. Whether or not you like it, people judge you not only on what you say, but how you say it. Even though we would like to think it shouldn't matter—that people should only judge us on the content of our character—the truth is that people do care and they do judge you. If you don't communicate well, their judgments of you may affect how they react toward you and how they treat you. They may not know exactly why they don't take to you or can't relate to you, but that "four-second" impression is lasting.

When it comes to our communication skills, we do not live in a democracy. Studies have shown that if you don't speak well, it will be harder to get people to respond positively to you. That can translate into not getting the job you want, the friends you want, or the mate you want. Research demonstrates that if you speak well, people will perceive you as being more intelligent, more sexually exciting, more competent, wealthier—and, yes, even less likely to have committed a crime.

My own research, which was the basis of my doctoral dissertation at the University of Minnesota, and currently a landmark study in the area of perception of speech and cosmetic appearance, clearly demonstrated that the way a person speaks is even more important than the way a person looks.

In fact, people with deformities may not be perceived as being physically attractive, but when they have attractive speaking voices, their speech overrides their looks. They are perceived as being attractive and appealing. I found this to be the case while doing my postdoctoral training at Harbor–UCLA Medical Center. As part of my research, I interviewed thousands of people who had such birth defects as dwarfism, neurofibromatosis (Elephant Man's disease) and numerous other genetic disorders (like the hero of the movie *Mask*, Rocky Dennis, who was my client). I found that those who spoke better lived better lives than those who didn't.

ATTRACTING TERRIFIC PEOPLE WITH THE OUTER YOU

You don't have to look like a model or a hunky movie star to attract terrific people. In fact, without the right makeup, hairstyle, and clothes, most models don't look like models. There is no doubt that the way in which you present yourself physically is important in terms of attracting someone initially; but if you are going to attract really great people to your life, you have to use a lot more than your looks alone.

Nobody can really tell you how to dress and what to wear. Most fashion is a matter of personal taste. Fashion is arbitrary and it will change depending on the climate in which you live, the culture of your locale, and the lifestyle you lead. You may dress differently depending on your mood, to make a statement, or to be noticed. Your fashion statement is in a state of constant change. In this day and age, where styles change daily, if you look put together, practice good hygiene, smell good, are well groomed, and dress appropriately to the situation, people will generally perceive you positively when making their first impression of you.

Attracting Potential Terrific People with a Smile and a Warm Hello

So many terrific people go unmet because other terrific people are too shy or too embarrassed to make the first move.

There is a simple remedy to this anxiety—just do it! Go up to the next person you would like to meet, smile, and say hello. It is that simple.

What is the worst thing that could happen? If you are rejected, you walk away with nothing more than a bruised ego. But when you stop and think for a moment, you realize that people who treat others in this fashion truly have the ego problem. If they had healthy egos, they would acknowledge you as a fellow human being. If you consider meeting new people from this perspective, you will never have to worry and feel inhibited about going up to people you find attractive and greeting them warmly.

I am not just sitting in an ivory tower spouting advice. I actually do what I suggest to you myself. The results are that I constantly meet wonderful, exciting people wherever I go.

In addition to my office in Los Angeles, I just opened a practice in Manhattan so that I could be available to clients on both coasts. Before I came to New York, people warned me about how unfriendly and rude New Yorkers could be and how I would have a hard time meeting people. New Yorkers have a reputation for being tough, rude, and self-centered. That certainly is not what I have observed. I found New Yorkers to be some of the warmest, loveliest, friendliest, helpful, and accommodating people in the world. Again, it is a matter of perspective; if you "in-vision" great people in your life, you will find them wherever you go. If you are receptive, you will generally be well received.

Every time I see people I would like to meet, I look right at them, smile, and say hello. Granted, some people may be taken aback, but most return my smile and start up a conversation with me. In addition, whenever I see someone looking at me, with friendly interest, I acknowledge that interest by smiling at them and saying hello. Interestingly, doing this can also help to deter any potential attackers. Studies have shown that potential assailants are less likely to harm a person who was friendly to them and made initial eye contact. Therefore, a mere hello may be your best form of self-defense.

ATTRACTING TERRIFIC PEOPLE BY THE WAY YOU SPEAK—IT'S NOT WHAT YOU SAY, IT'S HOW YOU SAY IT!

According to a recent Gallup Poll I commissioned, there are six main reasons people may be turned off by your speaking voice. You either:

1. Can't be heard because you are talking too softly and mumbling

2. Have a lifeless, boring, monotonous tone

3. Always use fillers like "um," "like," and "you know"

4. Have a nasal whine

5. Talk too fast, or

6. Have a voice that is too high pitched.

In this section, I will address each of these problems and give you pointers on how to correct these "talking turnoffs." If your voice is good, you are one step ahead on the path to finding fabulous people.

In all of the abovementioned cases, there is not only a physical component to these problems, but also a psychological component. Galen, the ancient Greek physician of the second century, was the first to recognize this. He stated that it was not the eyes that mirrored the soul, but rather the voice and speech. After working with many clients throughout the years, I clearly see how true this is. What goes on in your head and your heart is often mirrored in your voice.

Often, just a simple awareness of how to use your vocal cords and muscles properly may be all that is needed to produce good speech. In many cases, though, there may be strong psychological components that need further exploration before you can correct the situation, since what goes on in your head and heart comes out through your voice and speaking patterns; like too-rapid speech, too loud a voice, too soft a voice, too high a pitch, repeating words, and many other communication problems.

Should you need further assistance in rectifying your particular problems, I urge you to contact a therapist or qualified mental-health professional. Or you may contact me at either of my offices—the phone numbers and addresses are provided at the end of this book in the section "Where to Get Additional Information."

They Can't Hear You—Stop Mumbling

How can people connect with you or relate to you if they can't hear you? There is nothing more frustrating than to talk to people and not receive their entire message. You may ask them to repeat what they just said, and find yourself becoming more and more irritated. Eventually, whenever you enter a conversation with them, you either tune them out and stop listening or become impatient. Needless to say, your impatience will be reflected in your vocal tones and the way you respond to them, which will make them all the more self-conscious and will reinforce this negative cycle.

Often, people who mumble or who speak softly have low self-esteem. They just don't feel worthy of being heard. They also may not know the physical mechanics of good speech. Improving your self-esteem is also a key step to improving your attractiveness to others. Improving your speech is a big leap in the right direction.

Rx for Mumbling

If you suffer from a voice that nobody seems to hear, first consult an ear, nose, and throat specialist and get your hearing tested. Often people who have auditory-nerve damage speak too low. If you have already seen the physician or have had your hearing tested by an audiologist who has ruled out sensorineural deafness, then you need to do the following exercises. They will improve your use of air when speaking, helping you to project your voice and be heard.

Breathing-Out Technique

This exercise will increase your phonation time, which means increasing the length of tone you sustain on one breath. It is also designed to help you become more conscious of using your abdominal muscles when you speak.

1. While pushing out your abdominal muscles, sip in a breath of air for two seconds through your mouth. Be sure not to move your upper chest or your shoulders as you inhale.

2. Hold your breath for two seconds and then slowly exhale the air from your mouth for a count of approximately ten seconds. Repeat this exercise five times.

4. Next, repeat Steps 1 through 3, only this time say "ah" for as long as possible. Instead of exhaling air, you are now letting the air out of your mouth by saying "ah" on that continous stream of air.

5. Repeat Steps 1 through 4, only this time say "ah" for five seconds. Now, glide into an "oo," and continue making the sound for another five seconds, while still using the same breath you used when saying "ah."

This entire sequence will take thirteen seconds as you: rapidly sip the breath in through your mouth for one second, hold the air in your mouth for two seconds, then slowly and gently let out the "ah" for five seconds on a smooth airstream through your mouth. Now immediately change the "ah" sound to an "oo," all the while using the same breath for an additional five seconds.

Repeat this exercise five more times.

Coordinating Your Breathing with Your Speaking

Most people who have a problem being heard do so because they don't have enough air to sustain them when they speak, because they don't speak on their exhaled breath. Instead, they let all the air out immediately before they start to talk as though they are sighing, and thereby speak on little or no air at all. Because there is little or no airstream on which to project their words vocally, their voices do not carry and cannot be heard. They also tend to take in too many little breaths of air, which is not only exhausting, but also doesn't allow for good projection. These exercises will help you marry your breathing to your speaking.

1. Take a breath of air in through your mouth for one second.

2. Hold it for one second.

3. Then speak for as long as you can on that one breath until you run out of air. Take your time as you speak. Don't rush the words out. Repeat this exercise over and over again until it becomes incorporated into your regular speaking pattern. Speaking like this consistently allows you to be heard, gives you the time to think about what you're going to say before you say it, slows you down so that you don't speak so rapidly, eliminates choppiness by increasing smoother airflow and, finally, gives you more control when you speak.

Using Abdominal-Muscle Support for Projecting Your Voice

Just as you need the proper airflow and the proper coordination of your speech and airflow to be heard, you also need to use your abdominal muscles to help support your voice when you speak. With proper use of these muscles, you will have a louder voice because you will be forcing your large abdominal muscles to the work instead of taxing the smaller, weaker muscles of your throat.

The next three exercises will help you to strengthen and develop better use of your abdominal muscles and thus improve your projection when you speak.

CHAIR PUSHES AND PULLS

1. Sit in a chair and try to pull up on the sides of the chair as you remain seated.

2. Next, pull and release your pull five times in succession while saying "ah" for as long as you possibly can. You will feel the tone coming from your abdomen as you feel a slight pressure or a slight pull there. You will also hear a wavering sound as you alternately pull up on the chair and release your grip, all the while saying "ah."

3. Now, instead of pulling up on your chair, push down on the sides of the chair as you say "ah" while alternately pushing and releasing your push five times in succession. Once again, you will hear a wavering sound and feel a slight movement of your abdomen, similar to what you heard and felt in Step 2, when you said "ah" as you alternately pulled up on the chair and then released your grip.

HANDCLASPS

1. Interlock your fingers and extend your elbows so that they are parallel with your chest.

2. Now try to pull your interlocked fingers apart as you say "ah" for as long as you can. You will notice that the sound is louder and richer when you grip your fingers together than when you release your grip.

3. Next, release your grip while saying "ah." You will notice that the "ah" is softer than in Step 2.

4. Next, continue saying "ah" for as long as you can while alternately pulling and releasing your interlocked fingers. You will hear the tone alternately get louder and softer, which may result in a wavering tone as you pull and release your grip. In addition, you will feel a slight pressure in your abdomen, where the muscles will tighten and relax. As your muscles relax when you release your grip, the tone gets softer. As you tighten your grip and try to pull your fingers apart, there is more pressure in your abdomen and the tone becomes louder.

5. Do this five times, alternately pulling and releasing your grip.

ABDOMINAL BOUNCES

1. Slip in air through your mouth for two seconds.

2. Hold the air in your mouth for two seconds.

3. Now put your right hand on your abdomen just below your breastbone and say ''ha'' three times in succession on one breath. (i.e., ''ha ha ha'').

4. You will feel the tone vibrating in your abdomen as you feel slight pressure there. You will also notice that your abdominal muscles are pushed outward instead of inward as you say the ''ha ha has'' in succession. In addition, the tone is louder when your abdominal muscles are pushed out.

5. Repeat five times.

These three exercises will help you to focus on your abdominal muscles. If you push your abdominal muscles out when you speak and feel a little pressure in that area when you talk, you will have more vocal control and people will be able to hear everything you have to say. They will also have more confidence in what you have said, which, in turn, will help increase your self-confidence.

Rx for Sounding Dead, Boring, and Monotonous

Nobody wants to talk to a person who sounds dull and lifeless. You can be in the greatest mood, but if you don't reflect your passion or your enthusiasm through your voice, nobody else will know. In fact, based on your vocal response, listeners may feel that you are unenthusiastic or uninterested.

Roy met a woman with whom he was completely infatuated, but she never knew it because every time he spoke with her over the phone, his dull and lifeless tones indicated that he had no interest in her. The lack of encouragement in his tone turned her off, and her lack of response to him subsequently turned him off. As a result, they never got together, and another potentially great relationship never happened.

After working with Roy and teaching him the following exercises, he became more conscious of expressing his emotions through his voice. Several months later, he ran into the same woman. He spoke to her now with newfound zest in his voice, and her eyes lit up. The chemistry between them sparked, and as of my last communication with Roy, they are still dating. She got the message he was interested because he finally communicated that message through his tones.

Now, when Roy tells her "I love you," he says it with a tone of conviction, passion, and warmth.

The next two exercises are designed to help you put more emotion and flexibility in your voice.

UP/DOWN GLIDE TECHNIQUE

1. Sing the first three notes of a scale on "do," "re," "mi," Sing these notes without straining, making sure that your voice is comfortable and relaxed as you sing.

2. Next, slide the "do" vowel down the scale for two notes singing "me." Feel comfortable and do not strain your voice.

3. Now sing "do" "re" "mi" up the scale and mi" "re" do" down the scale on one breath.

This exercise is designed to help your vocal muscles become more flexible as you practice adding emotion and inflection when you speak to others.

THE EMOTION EXERCISE

Say "ah" while expressing the following ten emotions. Don't be afraid to let yourself go. In order to convey these different emotions, try to recall feeling a certain way in the past. Try to remember the feeling of what it was like when you didn't get the job you were right for, or when you were madly in love with someone, or when you were sitting in a classroom absolutely bored to death. Use a tape recorder to record yourself saying "ah" as you express the emotion. As you listen to the tape, pay close attention to whether you are gliding up or down as you say "ah" while reflecting that particular emotion. Say "ah" as you feel and express:

1. Sadness

2. Surprise

3. Anger

4. Happiness

5. Fear

6. Sympathy

7. Love

8. Disgust

9. Boredom

10. Doubt

Did you notice that when you sounded sad or bored, your tone was flat, and the duration of the tone was short? When you were excited, happy, and in love, your tone was upbeat and the duration of the sound was longer? Did you notice that when you showed sympathy, the tone glided down, but it was a lot softer than when you demonstrated anger.

Doing this exercise will help you to incorporate these sounds vocally into your daily conversations with others. Many people object to "wearing their emotions on their sleeve." Well, don't do that—wear them where they belong, in your voice. When you speak to someone, express your emotions freely. Don't sound like a computer or a robot. Instead, show some life when you talk because life is filled with emotion. When you like someone, let it show in your voice. When you are upset, let it out vocally. Feeling one way but sounding another is not only confusing to your own psyche, but is even more confusing to the person to whom you are talking. For example, if you you tell people that you are angry with them and not to do something again a soft monotonous tone, it is unlikely that they will understand how you really feel. They will probably think that you weren't that serious and that everything is fine. On the other hand, if you express your anger through a louder, flatter, more clipped tone, they will probably get the message and not repeat their mistakes.

You need to express your emotions so that people understand you mean what you say.

Rx to Stop Killing a Conversation with Fillers— "Like," "Um," "You Know."

It is completely disconcerting to listen to people who pepper their speech with "like," "um," "you know," and "uh."

I once had a college professor who used to say "like . . . um" and "you know" throughout his lectures. It was so distracting that it became laughable. The students used to have contests at the end of each class to see how many "like," "um," and "you knows" the professor said during the course of the hour. Needless to say, it was certainly difficult to concentrate on the topic of the day.

Not only is it distracting to use fillers, but it can give others the wrong impression that the person isn't very sharp or bright. Unfortunately, for too many teenagers and young people, it has become popular to speak using this lingo. But when reality hits and they have to make a good impression to find a job or get into a good school, they often realize that this ''street talk'' isn't so hip and cool, after all. Here are some helpful ways to eliminate the fillers from your speech:

1. Get a small hand-held tape recorder so that you can record your speech spontaneously in different situations.

2. Play back the tape and count the number of times you use the filler words. No matter how uncomfortable it is to listen to the tape, you need to do this. You cannot eliminate or reduce a bad habit until you are aware of how frequently you do it.

3. Whenever you speak, try to be mindful of what you are saying—and how you are saying it. Just being aware and focused on the problem will help you to reduce the numbers of fillers you use in your speech.

4. Substitute the ''um,'' ''like,'' and ''you know'' with a breath. Breathe in through your mouth for a second, hold it, and then begin to speak.

Doing these exercises will help you to control your use of filler words. Don't get frustrated if it doesn't happen right away. Be patient and consistent in monitoring yourself, and continue substituting breaths of air for filler words. Remember that the more you practice, and the sooner you are conscious, the quicker you will eliminate this problem. This technique is also excellent for eliminating swearwords or cursing from your vocabulary.

Rx for Losing the Nasal Whine

Unless you are Fran Drescher of *The Nanny* fame and have the number-one sitcom in the country, are internationally famous because of your nasal whine, and have written the best-selling book *Enter Whining,* you must get rid of your nasal-sounding voice forever. (I was the Dr. Glass whom Fran wrote about in her book in the chapter titled ''The Rain in Spain.'')

When Fran began her career, I worked with her to help her eliminate that severe nasal tone. When she first walked into my offices, I thought someone was playing a joke on me. I thought that she was actually goofing on me, putting me on with that shocking tone. I thought to myself that there was no way such a breathtakingly beautiful woman could sound like that. So I immediately burst out laughing as I said, ''All right, enough is enough. Who put you up to this?'' When I saw that Fran wasn't laughing, I almost died of embarrassment. I don't laugh at clients who come to me for help. She then told me that everyone wanted her to lose her accent so that she could get more work in Hollywood. Although it was a challenge, we accomplished the results in record time, and soon Fran had the sexiest, most sensuous, elegant, perfectly articulated, and well-modulated voice ever imaginable. She was my best-success story—until she discovered that she couldn't get work in Hollywood without her nasal whine. So she went back to her old ways, and the rest is an American success story.

For most people, hearing a nasal voice annoys them so much that they find the whiner difficult to take for long periods of time. In fact, the Gallup Poll I mentioned earlier in this chapter showed that close to 70 percent of the people surveyed found a nasal voice to be incredibly off-putting.

Unless they were born with a deformity of the palate, most people sound nasal because they don't open their mouths wide enough when they speak. They may start out speaking with an open, relaxed jaw, but they close their jaws as they continue to speak, so that they become nasal. The next two exercises can help you eliminate this nasal quality from your voice:

THE IMAGINARY-PENCIL EXERCISE

This exercise will help you feel the difference between sounding nasal and not (when you hear and feel a buzzing tone in your nose and when you do not). When you speak, pretend that you have the eraser at the top of an imaginary pencil placed between your back teeth, propping your jaws open. In reality, this is the exact position your jaws should be in when you are speaking in a normal, relaxed tone. It is called your normal "rest position."

1. Still imagining the eraser, keep your jaws propped open and make certain that the back of your teeth aren't touching.

2. Place your middle finger and your thumb on the bridge of your nose.

3. Say "ba, ba, ba, ba, ba" on one breath of air.

4. Now clench your jaws together so that your back teeth touch.

5. Repeat Steps 2 and 3 with your jaws clenched.

In the first three steps, you should not feel a nasal buzzing, while in the fourth and fifth steps, you should. This exercise clearly illustrates the importance of opening your jaws when you speak in order to avoid sounding nasal.

JAWING EXERCISE

This exercise further aids you in opening your jaws and in getting rid of nasal tones. It also helps you learn how to speak using the muscles in your mouth—instead of your nose:

1. Open your jaws and pretend that you are chewing out the following sounds ten times in succession:

a. ya ya ya ya ya ya ya ya ya

b. yo yo yo yo yo yo yo yo yo yo

c. ye ye ye ye ye ye ye ye ye ye

d. yoo yoo yoo yoo yoo yoo yoo yoo yoo yoo

In addition to reducing nasality, this exercise can also help you reduce mumbling, since you are getting more air in when your jaws are open.

Rx for Lowering Your Vocal Pitch and Sounding Like an Adult

Regardless of whether you are a man or woman, people do not take you very seriously if you have a high-pitched voice. Studies show that a person with a high-pitched voice is perceived as being less credible, weaker, and not as intelligent or successful as a person with a lower-pitched voice. We can see this depicted clearly in many Hollywood films, where the high-pitched-sounding woman is regarded as a bimbo, not to be taken seriously. In fact, she is often laughed at and ridiculed.

How detrimental having a high-pitched voice was seen when Hollywood made the transition from silent films to "talkies." Silent-film star John Gilbert was laughed off the screen, never to perform again, when audiences who previously had worshiped him had a good laugh at his expense. Those women who fantasized about this sex symbol of the day were now turned off as they heard his thin, squeaky voice. Throughout the years, I have worked with hundreds of handsome Hollywood actors who couldn't get arrested until they learned to lower the pitch of their voices. When they did, the roles came pouring in.

The Betty Boop–type voice may sound adorable at age twelve, but it doesn't work for a woman in her thirties, let alone forties. Often, having a voice of this sort reinforces feelings of helplessness, insecurity, and a lack of confidence. When a grown woman has a baby-girl voice, it usually means that she hasn't grown up and isn't comfortable with her womanliness. Her voice reveals that she is still trying to stay that little girl who often uses her cuteness to manipulate people and situations.

Studies also show that women who have baby-girl voices are not listened to as often as those women with lower-pitched voices. Research by Professor Paul Ekman done at the University of California at San Francisco demonstrates that when people lie, their voices tend to get higher. This research correlates to that done by others who have found that people who speak at a higher pitch are judged to be less credible.

A lower-pitched voice is considered to be an asset for both men and women. They are perceived to be not only more honest, but also more intelligent, stronger, more powerful, more sensuous, and more sexy.

I know a woman who fell madly in love with a man just by the rich, deep, tones of his voice. It had a profound physical effect on her. It literally took her breath away. As she got chills from head to toe, her heart would start to pound and her breathing rate became deeper and more rapid—all signs of sexual arousal. (Many women who have listened to singer Barry White's albums can relate to how this woman felt when she heard this man's voice.)

If you want to sound more credible, sexy, and intelligent, this set of exercises will help you lower the pitch of your voice:

EXERCISE TO LOWER YOUR PITCH

1. Sing "do" "re" "mi" up the scale, holding each note for three seconds.

2. Next, sing "mi," "re," "do" down the scale, holding each note for three seconds.

3. Now sing these words down the scale to the tune of "mi," "re," "do"

a. Come

    see

       me.

b. Let

   it

     be.

c. I

  love

    you.

4. When you sing the last word on "do," draw it out for five seconds. For example: "I" (mi) "love" (re) "you" (do).

5. Repeat these exercises five times. Like most of the exercises discussed so far, you should do this exercise throughout the day; whenever you have a few moments of spare time when walking your dog, waiting for an elevator, driving, or when shopping.

When you speak in a conversation, try to speak on "do." Be sure to go down in pitch at the end of your sentences, not up. Unfortunately, too many people talk in what is called "uptalk": They raise their voices at the end of their sentences, which makes it sound as if they are asking a question instead of making a statement. Uptalk not only weakens your message, but it also confuses people. They may think you are asking a question, not making a statement.

In lowering your pitch, it is essential for you to remember to control your abdominal muscles by pushing out on them when you speak. This not only helps you to project the sound of your voice, but also helps you to deepen the your tone.

YOUR BODY TALKS, TOO!

The way you sit, stand, and walk all scream out valuable information about you: whether you are confident, comfortable with yourself, and comfortable with others. So much has been written about how certain body postures mean certain things, but most of what has been written is ridiculous. For example, years ago it was believed that if people crossed their arms in front of them while talking with you, it meant that they didn't like you and were closing you off. Now we realize that it could just mean that they are cold and are trying to keep warm, or that they are self-conscious about their breasts, or uncomfortable or self-conscious about their body weight. Because we have become more sophisticated and more savvy in "reading" people's body language, we have to realize the tremendous impact that it has on others with regard to how they perceive us in the world.

From the way we walk, to how we stand, to how we sit, to how we gesture, people are making decisions about us at every movement along the way, whether or not we like it. These tips are designed to help you move in a manner that clearly spells out self-confidence to others.

How to Stand

If we are hunched over, stand on one leg, or rock back and forth, are too stiff or too sloppy and too loose in our posture, we may give off a negative impression of ourselves. On the other hand, if we stand in a manner that reflects our feelings of importance, others will react similarly and treat us with more respect.

Recently there was a photograph in a national magazine that depicted President Clinton with all of the ambassadors from the United Nations. The most dramatic aspect of this photograph was that every single person had impeccable posture and stood in a manner that exuded enormous confidence. One could feel the power emanating from the people in this photograph. It said it all: Powerful people reflect their power in the way they carry themselves. They stand tall no matter how tall, short, or what shape their bodies are in—they know their worth is beyond such petty considerations.

In order to stand like someone who is self-confident, which will not only allow others to perceive you as being confident, but also will enable you to *feel* more self-confident, you need to do the following:

1. Pretend there is a string holding up the crown of your head.

2. Visualize that string running from the crown of your head to the base of your spine.

3. Look straight ahead.

4. Tighten your buttocks.

5. Roll your shoulders back.

6. Keep your arms relaxed at your sides.

How to Walk

You can tell a great deal about people just by the way they walk. Some people have aggressive walks, others have wimpy or tentative walks. Some have a bounce in their gait; others shuffle, waddle, or trot. Some even seem to drag themselves along. But the only walk which trumpets self-confidence is this one:

1. Start with the posture in the "Standing" exercise.

2. Walk at a steady pace—not too fast or too slowly.

3. Let your arms move freely and swing naturally as you walk.

How to Sit

Just as it is important to stand properly, it is equally important to sit in a manner that exudes confidence at all times.

1. Stand in front of your chair and let your calves touch the seat of the chair.

2. Next, bend and place your buttocks all the way back in the chair.

3. Then, sit and lean your back against the back of the chair. By placing your buttocks all the way back in the chair first, you will notice that your spine will straighten automatically as it rests against the back of the chair. Doing this also prevents you from slouching.

4. Roll your shoulders back and relax your arms. You may either rest your arms on the arms of the chair or place your hands in your lap.

5. Keep your head up. Visualize a string holding up the crown of your head. This will also help you to keep your eyes focused at the eye level of the person opposite whom you may be sitting.

6. If you feel yourself slouching or sitting sloppily, just remember to push your buttocks all the way back in the chair. Lean against the back of the chair and keep the crown of your head up.

THE ART OF THE GESTURE

One of the most common questions I am asked is "What do I do with my hands when I speak?" My answer is "Use them," but use them appropriately. You don't want to look like a flailing chicken; that can be very distracting to the listener. Instead, use your hands to emphasize important points, making deliberate, sure movements. If you use your hands when you speak and incorporate a more open arm and hand position, people will perceive you as being warmer and more accessible. A study done at Harvard University indicated that people feel greater rapport with physicians who use more hand and arm movements in communicating with their patients.

If you feel that you use your arms and hands too much when you speak, remember to be mindful. When you have the knowledge or the awareness that you are doing something wrong, you can stop it. If you are sitting, you may want to clasp your hands in your lap. If you are standing or walking, you may want to clasp your hands in back of you, as members of the British royal family do when they do their "walka-bouts." This can also suggest a sense of control, security, and self-assurance.

Your Handshake Makes an Immediate Impression

You may not even realize it, but people may never want to get to know you if your handshake turns them off. If your handshake is too strong and your grip is too tight, it reveals a lot of agression and competitiveness. On the other hand, if you have a wimpy handshake, in which you barely touch the other person, or you just lightly grip their fingers, it may indicate that you are shy, have no self-confidence, or don't like or care about the other person.

In order to avoid any of these problems, this is how to shake hands with assurance:

1. Be the first one to reach out your hand. Do it enthusiastically and confidently.

2. Firmly clasp the other person's palm with your palm. Do *not* be afraid to touch them.

3. Look right at the person's face, smile, and shake his or her hand firmly about three times.

4. Release your grip.

5. If you know the person and like him or her, or if you have just met and have had a good interaction and have "connected" or "bonded," place your left hand over your right hand, cupping his or her hand in both of yours. This will let the person know your warm feelings toward them.

TO TOUCH OR NOT TO TOUCH? THAT IS THE QUESTION

In this day and age where everyone is so conscious of sexual-harassment lawsuits, people seem to be terrified of touching anyone. It is an unfortunate repercussion of what is perhaps the most basic and human of our needs—the need to be touched. Famed anthropologist Ashley Montagu pointed out in his research on touching that we all need physical contact. As children we long to be touched, and we long to touch others. We didn't think twice about touching someone else to let them know how we felt about them. Unfortunately, as we got older, we tended to keep our distances and touched less.

Despite the frequency of sexual-harassment lawsuits, most people aren't going to sue you for touching them, providing that you have mutual respect for one another and don't touch them in inappropriate places. Most people touch one another to show a bond, a connection, warmth, and appreciation.

In fact most people enjoy being touched and react better to those who touch them. To illustrate this point, a study was done in the library of a major university. In the process of checking out books, the librarian either touched or refrained from touching a student. All the students who checked out books were then asked to answer a questionnaire rating the library personnel and facilities. The results showed that the students who were touched rated the librarians more positively than the students who weren't touched. Further research indicates that the more people are touched, the more positively they react toward the person touching them.

Touching bonds you to another person and helps to break down barriers. It even helps to diffuse tensions between people. Try placing your hand gently on a person's shoulder the next time there is a disagreement about something and there is tension between the two of you. Observe what happens to your adversary when you reach out and touch them. More than likely, you will notice that the tension will dissipate between the two of you.

Touching mainly lets you know that the other person likes you, has affection toward you, and is connected with you.

Rules for Touching

1. Never touch people who may not welcome your touches. Read their nonverbal body and facial cues.

2. Pay attention to how much you touch the person. Too much touching is as disturbing as not touching at all.

3. In business situations, never touch below the level of the shoulders and/or the lower back.

4. Socially, touch face, arms, waist, and wherever else you and the other person mutually agree is acceptable.

5. Make sure your grip isn't too tight or too lax.

YOUR FACE SPEAKS 1000 WORDS

Like your body, your face can tell a whole story about your life. You can often tell if people—especially older people— have had good lives or miserable ones, based on the way their facial muscles course. Does the mouth droop, indicating that they have had sad and/or mean expressions on their faces throughout their lives? Or does the mouth turn upward, because they have lived life optimistically?

The importance of your facial expression, its animation, and its effect on others is not a new concept. Charles Darwin wrote about it as early as 1872. He discussed how people with certain facial characteristics were perceived positively by others, while those with other facial characteristics were perceived negatively.

Your facial expression can create either a positive or a negative initial impression. The findings of team of psychologists and political analysts at Dartmouth College illustrate the impact that a person's facial expression has upon others' perceptions of them. They found that Ronald Reagan had an early advantage in his 1980 election campaign because of the emotional intensity and diversity of his facial expressions. Unfortunately, the study found that it didn't matter whether or not people agreed with his political view. Instead, it was his emotional expressiveness that caused physiological changes in the viewer's skin response and heart rates. Even more astounding, the researchers also found that those subjects who had previously not made up their minds ended up supporting Reagan after they watched the videotape.

This research shows us how powerfully our facial language impacts others. Because of our facial expressions, people may read us wrong and thus react negatively. Many people furrow their foreheads and knit their brows when they listen intently. But a viewer may misread the facial cue as a frown and may react defensively or even angrily, in an edgy, harsh, or abrupt voice. It may even inhibit people from opening up to you because they will perceive you as being judgmental or critical, when in reality you may just be listening intently.

Thus, it is essential for you to be conscious of your facial expressions at all times, making an effort to relax your facial muscles whenever you are speaking or listening to someone. Instead of furrowing your brows, try opening your eyes wider—this is often perceived as an expression of interest in what the person is saying. Instead of pursing your lips tightly when you are about to speak, which may give the impression that you are on the verbal attack, relax the muscles around your lips, and drop your jaw slightly open. Throughout your conversation, periodically release the tension in your forehead, in the muscles around your eyes, nose, lips, and jaw.

Don't just look interested when talking to others, *be* interested! You need to both listen carefully to what they are saying and look closely at how they are saying things. Watch their facial expressions and body posture as a barometer to indicate how they really feel about specific things like relationships.

Since approximately 75 percent of our nonverbal communication is done with our face, in order for you to get the correct message across to another person, you must be conscious and mindful of what your face is "saying." It is important that your face show the emotion you are feeling, so others don't misinterpret your intentions.

Face Contact

You have probably grown up hearing the old adage: "You can trust a person who looks you in the eye." This isn't necessarily so. A more accurate statement would be that you are more likely to relate to and connect with people who look at your *face* when they speak and listen to you. Just as animals may feel threatened or challenged when you stare into their eyes, so do many people. People can perceive looking directly into a person's eyes as an attempt to intimidate them. (Unless, of course, they are madly in love with that person). But, as uncomfortable as it is for many people to have another person staring into their eyes, or staring at them, it is equally disconcerting to have a person look away constantly. It is rude, insensitive, disrespectful, and unacceptable not to focus on—and fully give your attention to—the person with whom you are speaking.

The following example clearly illustrates just how objectionable it is. A client of mine was at a Hollywood party talking to a colleague who, while glancing around the room to find someone more important to speak to, managed to spew forth some cordialities by asking Sherol about her father. Sherol replied sadly, "My father died last month." Obviously not paying attention to her answer, he smiled and replied immediately, "Oh, that's nice. Look, I see someone I need to talk to—I'll catch you later."

Sherol was so flabbergasted that she never spoke to him again. This ignorant soul had no idea why Sherol refused to take his calls and to do further business with him.

Thus, in order to have great communication with others and to be perceived as being interested in them and what they have to say, this exercise is designed to help you feel comfortable while gazing at the people with whom you are talking—not making them feel "stared at," but paid attention to. Open your eyes and your ears, and listen to what they are expressing to you.

1. Look at the person's entire face for two seconds.

2. Next, look at their eyes for two seconds.

3. Move your gaze to their nose, mouth, and chin—looking at each for two seconds.

4. Now go back and glance at their entire face for two seconds.

5. Repeat Steps 1–3 throughout the conversation.

At first you may find this feels somewhat awkward, and your instinct may be to look away. However, as you continue to practice this technique, you will begin to feel more and more comfortable. In turn, the person to whom you are speaking will have better rapport with you and will perceive you as being more receptive and interested, which will encourage opening up and sharing more with you, and thereby establish a closer bond between you.

It's Not Just How You Say It— It's What You Say That Counts!

Just as it is essential for you to express your tones appropriately so that you won't be misread or misinterpreted, it is equally important to express yourself in words that are appropriate.

We all grew up hearing the nursery rhyme, "Sticks and stones can break my bones, but words can never hurt me." We all wanted to believe it, but the truth is that words can not only hurt you, they can maim your feelings, kill your spirit, and annihilate your self-esteem. Certainly children, in their lack of development of social etiquette, can be very cruel to others. What is even sadder, many of these children grow up to be nasty adults who are completely unconscious about how their words can affect others because no one ever teaches them differently.

Just as you have to be responsible and let people know when they hurt you, you also have an obligation as a responsible adult to be accountable for whatever comes out of your mouth. You just can't blurt things out randomly, speak ill of someone, say insensitive, blunt, and hurtful things, and expect others to forgive you and to relate to you as though nothing happened.

Other than your parents, nobody has to like you unconditionally. If you speak and behave insensitively to others, you have to be prepared to suffer the consequences.

In order to prevent verbal faux pas from occurring, or being insensitive to others, you must again be mindful of what comes out of your mouth at all times. Even if you think you are "joking," others may not perceive it as funny.

There is nothing more hostile and revealing about a person than to hear them make an ugly, sarcastic, snide, or hurtful comment about another, watch the target's face change to shock, and then say, "I was only kidding." This is unconscionable. If you have done this in the past, don't ever do it to anyone again. If you still do it, stop it immediately. There is nothing funny or "kidding" about hurting another person's feelings.

SHY PEOPLE ARE SELFISH PEOPLE

You are probably shocked by this statement, but if you think about it, you will realize that it is absolutely true. Shy people are so concerned about themselves and so conscious about what others think of them that they hide from others.

On the other hand, people who aren't shy are more concerned about you, how you are doing, what you are thinking, and what you are doing than with how they might appear.

In order to get over the epidemic of shyness (the number-one social disease in this country) you need to get the focus completely off yourself and truly shift it to others. In doing so, you will notice that you are too busy thinking about others to think about how stupid or awkward you may feel.

Because shyness is based on fear—the fear of what someone thinks of you—you consciously need to stop playing the *"I think that you think that I think"* game with yourself. When you stop caring what others think of you, it frees you to be yourself. If you are more concerned about being *interested* in them as opposed to being *interesting* to them, you won't lose sight of what you want to say to them, and you won't worry about what kind of impression you are making. If you ever find yourself feeling shy in any situation, say the following phrases to yourself. They will help you break the cycle of ever feeling insecure and uncomfortable around others again:

1. *I REFUSE TO PLAY THE "I THINK THAT YOU THINK THAT I THINK" GAME.*

2. *I AM INTERESTED—I DON'T HAVE TO BE INTERESTING.*

Blow Shyness Away!

Another technique to help you to reduce or to eliminate your shyness is to breathe it out. Practice this in private, just before going to a party, meeting, or other social engagement.

1. Take a small sip of air in through your mouth.

2. Hold that breath for a few seconds.

3. Now, with all your might, blow that air out in a steady stream until you run out of air.

4. Repeat Steps 1–3 until your nervousness is gone.

You have now calmed down to the point that you can get out of your own way. You can go up to people, meet, and greet them. Go for it! Don't think twice—do it!

How to Have a Great Conversation: What Do You Say After You've Said Hello?

To start a conversation off right, you have to say something to attract the other person's attention, whether it be in the form of an observation, a question, or a compliment. Compliments are perfect icebreakers and are the key to opening a conversation. Starting a conversation with "You look stunning in that dress—where did you get it?" can get you a response that can move the conversation along. She may tell you that she bought the dress in Europe. This gives you perfect entree into discussing Europe, where she has been, etc.

Making an observation is another opener. For example, if you are at a party, you could say, "Look at what a gracious hostess Mary is. She is always so sweet and friendly. Don't you think she always gives the best parties?" News events are also wonderful openers: "What do you think about so-and-so winning the election?" If you don't know what's going on in the world, scan the headlines of your newspaper, look at *USA Today,* which capsulizes the news in an easy-to-read manner, or turn on CNN for a few minutes to get the latest news.

I can't begin to stress enough the importance of being current and knowing what is going on in your world if you want to have something to discuss when you meet new people. The weather or traffic conditions are great openers, since people generally have these issues in common, and are almost certain to have opinions on them.

Whatever you do in starting a conversation, never—under any circumstances—make a sarcastic comment, put anyone down, or give anyone a "line." No one wants to be disrespected and flattered falsely. Instead, the best way to entice people into continuing to speak to you is by being respectful, honest, and forthright. If they respond cordially to your opening comment, they are signaling you to introduce yourself. Giving both your first and last name when you introduce yourself to someone indicates openness and generally elicits greater trust in the other person.

Maintaining the Conversation Involves Exploring Common Ground

In order for a conversation to continue, it is essential to find common ground. You can't talk to anyone for very long unless you have something in common. Ask questions that are open-ended instead of those requiring only "yes" or "no" answers; you will acquire more information about people, which in turn allows you to better relate to what they are talking about. Continue asking them questions; base your questions on their answers to what you asked them last. For example, let's say you ask people where they are from, and they say Los Angeles.

You then ask, "Where in Los Angeles?"

They answer, "Beverly Hills."

You say, "Beverly Hills? What was it like growing up there? Is it like what they depict on *90210?*" They may answer that it's not at all like the show, or that it has really changed a lot. You can then ask, "How so?" etc. The key is to keep engaging them in conversation so that you begin to establish a free-flowing momentum, so that they ask you questions and you ask them questions, and a give-and-take is established in which to learn about each other.

This technique of further engaging someone in conversation by asking is called "elaboration." It is much like what news reporters do when they ask questions to draw more information out of an interviewee. These *who, what, when, where, and why* questions tend to draw the person out and allow them to answer in a more descriptive manner. In continuing to engage a person in conversation, the key is to use as much description as possible when telling stories, relating experiences, and discussing events. People's interests are engaged by stimulating images. Using descriptive words and phrases, relaying visual and auditory images, and peppering your descriptions with your emotional reactions to the experiences makes the people to whom you are telling your story feel as though they were right there with you.

Don't Just Look and Hear—Observe and Listen

Being a great observer and a great listener enables you to make proper assessments about others. You can read them much better and really understand what they are communicating to you. Careful and active listening affords you the opportunity to ask deeper, more meaningful questions of the people with whom you speak, and to eliminate the superficiality of the relationship.

Your attentiveness to their facial and body cues tells you whether to continue with your questioning or to back off. Paying attention to visual cues, such as a wince or a frown, lets you know when you have touched on a particularly sensitive area. For example, after asking people where their parents live, you immediately notice some slight tension in their faces. Perhaps they lost a family member recently, or maybe they don't have particularly good relations with their parents. Whatever the case, your awareness of their facial cues lets you determine whether you have overstepped your boundaries and need to change the subject, or whether to continue on with the discussion.

Being a good listener is paramount to being a good conversationalist. In order to be a good listener, there are three basic things you need to remember:

1. Focus on the other person and talk about them, not about yourself. Bring your own experiences into the conversation only as they relate to the experiences of the other person. Unfortunately, too many relationships have gone awry when one person was trying to outdo the other in sharing his or her experiences. Communication is not a competitive event, but rather a sharing of ideas, information, and experiences as they relate to both parties involved.

2. Remember to maintain face contact throughout the conversation. Do not look away. It is equally important to focus all of your attention, at all times, on what the person is saying.

3. Don't interrupt, tune out, make judgments, or jump to conclusions, especially when you hear a word or concept to which you may have an emotional reaction or that you may find objectionable. Instead, let the person finish, so that you get the entire message and not just a small part of it. Then you can speak and share your comments, feelings, and experiences.

Ending the Conversation

Don't linger when it is time to go. If you are finished speaking with someone and are having a problem ending a conversation, there are some things you can do to transmit to the other person that it is about to close. This can be done without awkwardness and without hurting anyone's feelings.

1. Assuming that you have maintained good face contact throughout the course of the conversation, breaking that contact by looking off to the side or glancing in another direction will signal that the conversation is coming to an end.

2. End by saying, "It was so nice speaking with you," or "I enjoyed hearing what you had to say." If you are at a social gathering and want to meet other people, say something like "It was so nice to speak with you. I am going to mingle with some other people now. Perhaps we will see each other again." If you want to see the other person again, say something like, "Let's continue our conversation sometime soon," or "I'd love to see you again." This way you can exchange cards and phone numbers. Never be hypocritical. If you are not interested in seeing him or her again, you may just want to say, "Nice to meet you," and then leave.

When you leave people, remember that the final impression you make is just as important as the initial one. So leave on an upbeat vocal tone, give them a warm touch, hug, small kiss on the cheek, and a two-handed handshake (you cup their hands into both of yours). These gestures let them know how very much you enjoyed their company and how anxious you are to see them again.

Be a Diplomat at All Times!

Let's say you have met people who really aren't your cup of tea. You don't like their personalities, or you have nothing in common with them. You really don't want anything further to do with them, but you also know that being polite and courteous is the only respectful way to act. The bottom line is to never be rude or hurt others' feelings if you can help it.

Many men who date are guilty of unintentional unkindness when they misinterpret what it means to be polite. They may meet a woman to whom they are not particularly attracted. But to be "nice," they think it is OK to say, "I'll call you" when they have no intention of calling or seeing her ever again. *If you learn one thing from this book, it should be to never say or do anything unless you mean it!* Mean what you say and say what you mean. But say what you mean in a diplomatic, nonhurtful way. A much better approach is "It was good speaking with you," or "You seem like a nice person." These are not lies. She may very well be a nice person (for someone else). Anything is better than telling someone you will do something and then not doing it. You get their expectations up, and when you don't deliver, you not only come off as a bad person, but also an insensitive one.

Don't say anything you don't really mean. If you aren't attracted to people, or if they bore you, leave graciously and politely, allowing them to preserve their dignity.

Chapter 5

Becoming That Terrific Person to Yourself

- *Lies People Tell You*
- *Who Are You, Really?*
- *What Is the Good News About You?*
- *What Is the Not-So-Good News About You?*
- *What Can You Change About Yourself to Feel More Terrific?*
- *Tell Yourself the Good News Every Day*
- *To Know You Is to Love You*
- *Really Looking Through the Glass*
- *Talk Nicely to the Most Terrific Person You Know—You!*
- *The Power of the Word*
- *Don't Listen to Negative People—Always Trust Your Guts!*
- *The Body Never Lies!*
- *A Victim No More!*
- *Letting People Know When They Have Overstepped Their Bounds*
- *The Minute You See These People, Run the Other Way*
- *Dealing with the Pain of Rejection Without Self-Destructing*
- *Throw Away Your Burdens and Count Your Blessings*
- *Accept the Help—You Deserve It*

I am sure you have heard the expression, "Before you can love another person, you have to love yourself." Perhaps the great playwright Oscar Wilde summed it up best in the following quote: "To love oneself is the beginning of a lifelong romance."

Too many of us hear the words, but we don't really pay close attention to the meaning of this profound statement. Perhaps so many relationships are in trouble because people don't love, appreciate, and respect themselves before they attempt to do the same with others.

Earlier in this book, we discussed how all too often people suffer from self-loathing. They really don't like and respect themselves. Unfortunately, all too often it manifests itself as the Groucho Marx Syndrome—not feeling deserving of being with anyone who wants to be with them. The consequences are debilitating to everyone involved.

The reason that people are unkind, unappreciative, and disrespectful to others generally stems from beliefs about themselves that are hurtful—they feel they are not good enough, not smart enough and, as a result, not worthy enough. Who gave them this information? Who knows and who cares? Whether it was a parent, or a teacher, classmate, or even the pages of a fashion magazine that brought out these feelings of inadequacy, it doesn't matter. As an adult, you are responsible for your actions. No one else is to blame. But, you must learn to walk before you can run. So you must first address the self-damage before you can be terrific to others.

In this chapter you will learn how to repair your self-esteem and be that terrific person to the most important person in your life—You. To do this, you have to like yourself, and I will show you how to accomplish this monumental and life-changing task.

Before you can effectively change a negative opinion about yourself to a positive one, you need to examine who you are. What are your likes and dislikes? What do you want to change about yourself? You also need to reprogram how you see yourself *and* what you say to yourself. You need a new set of guidelines to follow for the rest of your life. And, finally, you need to know how to indulge and pamper yourself and learn to openly accept others' kind words, positive opinions, and assistance.

The techniques and suggestions described in this chapter are of paramount importance. You will feel deserving of having other terrific people in your life and be able to accept the wonderful things they can and will do for you openly and willingly. Being with a terrific person is not just about giving. It is about being able to receive as well. But before you can receive from others, you have to give to yourself.

LIES PEOPLE TELL YOU

"You're not good enough."

"You're not smart enough."

"You're not pretty enough." What the heck is enough, and who are they to decide? If you are old enough to read this book, you are old enough to stop blaming others and to look to yourself for the answers. If you examine things closely enough, you will find that you are in charge of you. Since you bought into those lies and gave them substance, it's up to you to put all the lies you heard about yourself out on the table literally and figuratively and address and conquer them.

This exercise is designed to help you do just that.

1. Get a pack of Post-Its. On each page, write down one negative comment you have heard about yourself.

2. Think back through your life to recall the people who said nasty things to you and about you.

3. After you have written these phrases or comments on separate pages, pull out the Post-Its containing the lies or nasty comments others made about you, and stick them onto the side of a garbage can.

4. One by one, pull each Post-It off the can and read it out loud.

5. Now read it again with a chuckle, or with laughter in your voice. You are laughing at how ridiculous the comment that was made about you truly is.

6. Next, rip up the pages as you continue to mock these comments. Do this until all Post-Its are ripped up and in the trash.

7. Look into the garbage can with all of the ripped-up pieces of paper and say the following out loud:

"I have ripped up all of your nasty comments, your false and wrong opinions of me, and your lies about me. I have placed them where they belong and where they will stay forever—in the garbage. They will either end up in a landfill or will be burned and recycled. In any case, these lies and comments—like the little pieces of paper they were written on—no longer exist in my life!"

WHO ARE YOU, REALLY?

In my books *Talk to Win* and *Say It Right*, I shared with readers a "Getting to Know You" survey I developed that has been very effective in helping my clients learn more about themselves. By answering a detailed questionnaire about their likes and dislikes, they were able to see how they really felt about certain things.

The following "Who Am I, Really?" survey digs much deeper and is an even more effective gauge to your true thoughts and feelings. After you fill out your answers, go back and read them. Pretend that you are meeting this person for the very first time. You may find yourself getting very introspective, as one thought will trigger another thought about your life and how you have lived it, how you see yourself, and where you are going. There are no right or wrong answers. This exercise is not meant to be invasive or to inspire a judgmental assessment. Instead, it is designed to help you learn and explore more about yourself.

Fill in the blanks with the first thought that comes to your mind. Don't try to edit what you feel would be the "right" answers. Instead, answer truthfully and from the heart:

My name is_____.
If I could change my name, it would
    be_____.
I am_____years old.
I wish I were_____years of age.
I live in_____.
I'd rather live in_____.
My family is_____.
The perfect family is_____.
I make my living_____.
I'd rather make my living_____.
Socially, I_____.
Socially, I would rather_____.
My friends are_____.
I wish my friends were_____.
The qualities I value the most are_____.
The people I always seem to meet are_____.
The person whom I would most like to meet
    is_____.
I love people who are_____.
I can't stand people who are_____.
My favorite person in the world is_____.

I love to dress_____.
I hate to dress_____.
I love going to_____.
I dread going to_____.
Financially, I am_____.
Financially, I'd rather be_____.
Physically, I am_____.
Physically, I would rather be_____.
I love to_____.
What makes me laugh is_____.
What makes me cry is_____.
It saddens me that_____.
I am disgusted by_____.
I could scream when_____.
My biggest pet peeve is_____.
What embarrasses me is_____.
I am suspicious of_____.
I am exhausted by_____.
I feel guilty about_____.
What makes me angry is_____.
I get frustrated by_____.
I am most confident when_____.
I am hurt by_____.
I am nauseated by_____.
What makes me laugh is_____.
I am frightened about_____.
I am cautious about_____.
I am jealous of_____.
I am shocked by_____.
I am anxious about_____.
I am bored by_____.
I am hopeful about_____.
I am overwhelmed by_____.
I am ashamed by_____.
I am attracted to_____.
I am repulsed by_____.
I am surprised by_____.

I am confident about_____.
I am furious about_____.
When I feel rejected, I_____.
When I am accepted, I_____.
I worry about_____.
I never worry about_____.
I usually put off_____.
I am excited about_____.
I am turned off by_____.
Others see me as_____.
I see me as_____.
When I meet a new person I like, I_____.
When I meet a new person I don't like,
    I_____.
An ideal friendship would be_____.
An ideal mate would be_____.
My mate is_____.
In one week, I want to_____.
In one month, I want to_____.
In one year, I want to_____.
In five years, I want to_____.
I would be the happiest person if_____.

WHAT IS THE GOOD NEWS ABOUT YOU?

My greatest accomplishment is_____.
My best asset is my_____.
I am proud of myself when I_____.
My greatest talent is_____.
The best thing I like about the way I look
    is_____.
The thing I like best about my personality
    is_____.

The thing I like best about my character
    is_____ .
My fondest childhood memory is_____ .
My fondest memory of my teen years
    is_____ .
My fondest memories as an adult are_____ .
Three positive adjectives to describe me are_____ ,
_____ ,_____ .

Good things I usually share with people
    are_____ .
I feel attractive when_____ .
I feel sexy when_____ .
I feel powerful when_____ .
The three best qualities about me are_____ ,
_____ ,_____ .

The best things I do for myself are_____ .
The greatest people I have surrounded myself with
    are_____ .

WHAT IS THE NOT-SO-GOOD NEWS ABOUT YOU?

My biggest regret is_____ .
The thing I hate the most about myself
    is_____ .
The thing I dislike most about my personality
    is_____ .
The thing I dislike most about my character
    is_____ .
The thing that people ''call me on'' the most
    is_____ .
The worst thing I do to myself is_____ .
The worst thing I did as a child was_____ .
The worst thing I did as a teenager
    was_____ .

The worst thing I do or have done as an adult
is/was_____.

I am insecure about_____.

I always worry about_____.

Three negative adjectives to describe me are_____,

_____,_____.

Negative things I usually share with people
are_____.

The worst people I have surrounded myself with
are_____.

WHAT CAN YOU CHANGE ABOUT YOURSELF TO FEEL MORE TERRIFIC?

Look carefully at all of the answers you gave concerning what you perceive as your negative traits. Now that you are well aware of them, go through all of these questions again, only this time ask yourself what steps you can take to transform these traits into more positive ones. Make a list of these steps and traits in a special notebook, and keep it handy at all times. Whenever you see these negative traits cropping up, look up the cure in your little notebook and follow these steps to change these negative traits.

My client Marcy did this exercise and found that it changed her life. It allowed her to laugh at herself and helped eliminate her anxiety. Marcy found that her most negative trait is taking all rejection personally, turning it inward, and feeling horrible about herself. To add to these horrible feelings, she overeats, gets angry, and wallows in the depression that follows.

One day Marcy called on a company to pitch a product. She had a contact there whom she had met years earlier, but now she couldn't seem to get through to him. Randy put her off, saying he would get back to her, and then did not return her calls. Feeling anger, resentment, and hurt cropping up, Marcy looked into her notebook. She found the page titled "Problems Handling Rejection" and read the following steps to herself:

1. Turn it into humor

2. Confront the situation head-on to find out what the problem is.

3. Go to another person who can help you. Find another door to open.

4. Find someone who has good rapport with the person who can sing your praises.

5. Realize that it is their problem, not yours.

6. Call someone who makes you feel good.

7. Breathe out negative feelings.

8. Stay away from sweets.

Marcy then wrote Randy this note: "If you aren't returning my calls because I offended your mother, let me apologize. If I have offended you or anyone else, let me apologize for that as well. If you are so exceptionally busy that you have no time whatsoever to take my call, let me urge you to take two minutes of your time, as it would be in your best interest to do so." Marcy sent off the letter and let any hurt feelings go by breathing them out. She then made two other calls and set up two more meetings. She placed a call to a dear friend in Connecticut who was thrilled to hear from her, and she stayed away from the Mars Bars and the Nestlé Crunches. Several days later, she received a call from Randy. They set up a meeting and she sold her product to him—as she continues to do.

TELL YOURSELF THE GOOD NEWS
EVERY DAY

Often, when we hear good news or when something great happens to us, we can't wait to call someone up and share it. This allows us to hear the good news all over again and to relive the moment. If you tell the good news to people who may be a little jealous or whose life is not going as well, you may run the risk of their not sharing your enthusiasm. They may even give you a barrage of reasons why your good fortune won't last. They may make comments that bring you down or that get you to think negatively.

Therefore, doing this "Tell Yourself the Good News" exercise is guaranteed to reinforce your good feelings about yourself daily. If you feel good about yourself every day and reinforce what is "right" about you, you will develop the self-confidence to go out in the world and have other successes.

"Tell Yourself the Good News" Exercise

1. As soon as something great happens to you—you met the person of your dreams, you got a promotion, you made a major sale, you invested correctly and received a lot of money—tape-record your excitement. (This is why I recommend carrying a small hand-held tape recorder with you at all times.)

2. If you don't have a recorder handy, call yourself up and leave a message on your answering machine. Express all of the exuberance you would if you were telling a close friend. If you don't have an answering machine, get one (especially for peak moments like this). It is important to record yourself the moment the good news happens so that you can hear the genuine excitement in your voice. When you come home, record your message onto a tape on which you have collected all the "good news" about yourself.

3. Every morning when you first get up, go to the mirror. Listen to your "good news about you" tape.

4. While continuing to look in the mirror, say the following affirmations:

> "Good things will continue to happen for me."
>
> "I am a winner."
>
> "I love living in happiness and excitement, and that is going to be what I will experience every day."
>
> "I have confidence in myself, and others will, too."
>
> "I know that I am a good person. Nobody can tell me otherwise."
>
> "I will be open to all new opportunities."
>
> "I will accomplish my dream and take all necessary steps to do so."
>
> "I am proud of who I am."
>
> "I genuinely like myself."
>
> "I will help someone today."
>
> "I will help myself today."
>
> "Today will be terrific."

One of my clients, Wayne, a former salesman who now owns several companies and is a multimillionaire, would do an exercise similar to this one. Each day he would look in the mirror and say in his southern drawl, "Wayne, are we gonna have a great day today and make some money? You bet we are. We're gonna be happy and have a lot of fun making a lot of money."

His little mantra motivated him to the point that he felt so good about himself and so confident that he took more and more risks that further enhanced his self-worth so much so that his financial worth finally mirrored his self-worth.

To Know You Is To Love You

When I was in high school, I attended a sweet sixteen party at which a wonderful little white hand-held mirror was the party favor. The back of the mirror was shaped like a daisy, with white petals and a yellow center. The front of the mirror had writing on it that said "To know me is to love me." I loved that mirror because every time I looked into it, it reminded me that I should love myself. It made me think of and appreciate all my good qualities. Perhaps every mirror we look into should be equipped with this sign on it. But since this isn't possible, the next best thing is to make up a sign that says the same thing and stick it on the mirror you use the most. It will give you a boost and put positive thoughts into your mind.

Really Looking Through the Glass

If you don't feel good about yourself, your mind's mirror is either smudgy, cracked, or distorted. The following technique uses a real mirror as a tool to help you unsmudge, repair, and straighten out the mirror in your mind—the one that reflects negative and toxic thoughts about yourself back to you. In doing this exercise, your eyes and your ears will see and hear the good in you, which will make you begin to believe, accept, and radiate this feeling to others.

The Mirror Technique

This is a continuation of the "Tell Me Good News" exercise. Instead of doing this every morning, do it whenever you pass a mirror. You can do it when you are in front of a mirror at home, when you are in an elevator, when you pass a mirror on the street, when you are shopping and are trying on clothes in the mirror, or when you pass by a glass building and see your reflection.

1. Without speaking out loud, tell yourself your innermost dream or desire (i.e., I want to get married).

2. Next, give yourself a positive affirmation. (I will get married soon.)

3. Then say something great about yourself. (I have a lot to give, and I am loving and giving.)

Sometimes just seeing your reflection and saying something positive about yourself will give you an extra jolt to put you in an even better mood and in great spirits as you go about your day.

Marlena, one of my clients, credits meeting her husband through use of this mirror technique. Each day she would look into the mirror and tell herself how attractive she was, how beautiful her figure looked, how sweet she was, and what a wonderful person she was. Each time she went out in the evening, she looked in the mirror and said, "Marlena, you are the best, you are beautiful, and you will meet a wonderful man who will fall in love with you and be committed to you. You will be married this year." Ten months later, Marlena was married to a wonderful man. I was her maid of honor.

TALK NICELY TO THE MOST TERRIFIC PERSON YOU KNOW—YOU!

How can you expect others to speak nicely to you, or to treat you with respect if you speak ill of yourself and don't treat yourself with the respect you deserve?

This happened to an actress client of mine who went around constantly telling everyone how she hated her hair—until one day it caught up with her. While attending a party, she ran into a casting agent for commercials. When she left the vicinity, another agent asked this agent if he would consider using "the beautiful woman to whom he was just speaking" for the commercial he was presently casting.

The casting agent replied, "No, her hair is too messed up." Her hair wasn't messed up. The only thing messed up about her was the negative way she spoke about herself to others. People picked up her negative thoughts and words and followed her lead. If she spoke ill of and about herself, they felt free to do the same. Hence, the nonresults of her efforts to network a Hollywood party.

When you make statements like "I'm so fat," or "I'm so dumb," or I'm a jerk," other people will usually follow suit because they think that you know yourself better than anyone else does. If you think you are fat, then you probably are. If you think you are a jerk, then you're probably that, too.

Learn to say sweet and loving things to yourself. For example, when you drop a glass of water or spill something on the floor, don't call yourself names or say it was dumb, stupid, or clumsy. Talking to yourself in this way is verbal self-abuse. Instead, be kinder to yourself and say, "That's Okay, sweetheart," or "Don't worry, honey." It is important to speak to yourself using terms of endearment like: "honey," "sweetheart," "darling," "love," "angel," and "baby." Say these same things to yourself using the same loving tone that you would use to speak to someone you adore and respect.

If you say negative things to yourself like "I can't do this" or "That's just my luck," or "I never get anything right," you are headed toward fulfilling those self-created prophecies. On the other hand, saying things like "I'm gonna make it" or "It's gonna happen," will program your mind to focus on these things in a positive way. We all know about the power of positive thinking—it turns into positive action and creates a wonderful ripple effect in your daily encounters with others.

THE POWER OF THE WORD

I am a firm believer in the power of the word. What you say is who you are and what you will bring to yourself and others in life. Your brain needs to hear healthy thoughts to nourish and feed your soul. If you keep telling yourself how great, wonderful, and fabulous you are, not only will you begin to believe it, you will begin to live it. That is what happened to nineteen-year-old Cassius Clay from Mississippi. As he became a professional fighter, he brazenly broadcast his greatness to the world. He knew his talents and was very confident about his abilities in the ring. As obnoxious as it may have seemed to some, he knew that he was the greatest, and he let everybody else know it, too. He went on to become Muhammad Ali, the most respected heavyweight boxer in the world.

If you believe it, say it, and keep saying it to others, it will come to pass. I don't believe in the superstitiousness of not talking about something before it happens. Speak—and speak positively and excitedly and knowingly. Good things have a greater chance of happening because you may draw the positive to you through your enthusiasm.

DON'T LISTEN TO NEGATIVE PEOPLE— ALWAYS TRUST YOUR GUTS!

Have you ever thought that you should do something, but you ended up not doing it because you listened to someone—and lived to regret it?

On the other hand, have you ever done something despite others telling you not to do it, and giving you every possible warning—but you went ahead and did it anyway, and it turned out to be the best thing ever?

That is what happened to Sarah. She worked for a mediocre magazine, but wanted to work for a better one and obtain a better position. At a party, she met a man who was the editor-in-chief of a major publication. She was dying to talk to him, but her friends tried to dissuade her with comments like "He would never meet with you. You are just setting yourself up for rejection." Despite these statements, Sarah left her table and went over to talk to him. They hit it off, and today she works as an editor at one of the top women's magazines in the country.

This is called trusting your instincts, or "knowingness." It is knowing that you know what you know. Deep inside, you know the truth of what makes you happy, and what you need to do to achieve this in just about every situation. Just pay attention and listen to your inner voice to keep from getting into trouble. Listening to that inner voice and acting on it will make terrific things continue to happen in your life. It keeps you true to your inner core—and who you really are.

When heiress Ann Miller gave up her multimillion-dollar fortune, her world of celebrity friends, international travel, mansions, jewels, and designer clothes, everyone thought she had lost her mind. However, she knew better than anyone else what she was doing. All her privileged life, she always believed that there was something more for her. She knew that this calling was not about money. For her it was about spiritual growth and inner peace. Nobody could tell her differently. She trusted her instincts. After taking a vow of poverty and becoming a Carmelite nun, she has never been happier and more fulfilled.

THE BODY NEVER LIES!

Your body never lies, so pay close attention to it. Don't just listen to your head and your values; listen to your body for cues to what is right or wrong. Your body can serve as a barometer to let you know whether you should or shouldn't do something.

Keith, a physician, was offered a job at a hospital across town. He would be earning $20,000 more a year, and it was close to his home. In his new position, he would be involved in teaching medical residents, a job that he thought he'd love doing.

When he came into my office and told me about the new job he was planning to take, his voice sounded dull and morose. It wasn't the voice of a man ready to take on the world, let alone a new position. As I pointed this out to him, he opened up and told me that ever since he had received the job offer, he hadn't been able to sleep, had lost weight (he couldn't keep food down), had broken out in a rash, and had constant headaches.

I told Keith not to take the job since his body was clearly telling him not to. A smile came over his face as he said, "I guess I really don't want the job because I am so aware of all of the politics that go on in the department. And I am dreading having to work with the man who would be my boss because I know that he will make my life a living hell."

As soon as another client of mine became engaged, she developed an eye tic and migraine headaches. It was amazing how, three months later, after she broke off her engagement, the eye tics and migraines disappeared miraculously. Her body was screaming "no" to this man—whom she later found out was a chronic gambler and was in severe debt.

How to Listen to Your Guts and Trust Your Instincts

This is how to listen to your guts and trust your instincts:

1. Examine your breathing. Is it heavy or labored, or do you find yourself taking in many little shallow breaths? These are signs of tension and anxiety. Often, during stress, the upper chest muscles tense, creating irregular breathing patterns like these.

2. Pay attention to your facial tension. Are you frowning or tensing up areas around your mouth and lips? Are you furrowing your brow or forehead?

3. Examine your voice. Is it more high-pitched, indicating tension in your neck and throat muscles? Is it too loud, or do you attack the beginning of the sentence with a sudden loud burst? This may indicate tension and a feeling of helplessness and lack of control. Do you speak too softly, indicating insecurity and reduced self-confidence? Do you sound sad, boring, slow, monotonous, and lifeless, indicating that you are not very happy or feel doomed to failure?

4. Does your skin feel tingly, clammy, or break out in rashes? Have you had a sudden hair loss? Your autonomic nervous system may be warning you about something you shouldn't be doing.

5. Do you have stomach pains, headaches, chest pains? Like many people, you may internalize all of your stress, which has to come out in some way. Unfortunately, it may come out in the form of diarrhea, migranes, or blood-flow problems that result in strokes or heart attacks.

6. Do you have headaches, neck aches, or nervous tics? People often hold their stress in the face, neck, and back. If you have sudden pain in these areas when you did nothing to strain these muscles (playing sports or lifting heavy objects), you may be externalizing your stress and anxiety in these physical areas.

7. Do you find that you forget things and do not do things you are supposed to do? Your mind may be on overload due to the back-and-forth stress of attempting to weigh all of your options and come up with the right decision. Therefore, your mind shuts down or, figuratively, skips a few beats in order to deal with the enormous stress.

8. Examine your energy level. Do you feel drained and want to sleep all the time? This may indicate that your body is on overload and senses that a serious problem is about to happen. Therefore, it avoids confronting it. Your body may also be exhausted from inner conflict you are going through in trying to make a decision.

A VICTIM NO MORE!

Every time I appear as a guest on talk shows, I inevitably meet some of the most frustrating human beings in the world. No matter what advice I give them, they just "don't get it." They don't realize that they and nobody else are responsible for their actions. It is up to them to make certain decisions, to set certain limits, and to make positive things happen. They must realize that there are choices in life. You don't have to stay with someone who cheats on you or abuses you physically or mentally.

I have come to the conclusion that many people just love living in "victimville." They refuse to believe that they are not victims, that they can take responsibility for leading a good life. When generous and committed Geraldo Rivera offers to give teenagers a four-year scholarship to any college—and pay for it out of his own pocket, because he believes so strongly in their getting an education, so that they can get off the streets and better their lives—and they refuse, I want to scream.

When Gordon Elliott opens his big heart to tell people he's going to pay for their therapy, help them get their lives together, and they refuse, I want to throw up my hands in defeat.

It's like the old saying: "You can lead a horse to water, but you can't make it drink." All the help in the world cannot get victims out of "victimville" unless they want to get out.

Being a victim *doesn't* work. And, unfortunately, people will continue to victimize you if you allow them to. If you set no limits and feel you have no choices, and refuse to accept any assistance, you will indeed remain a victim. As you wallow in self-pity, others will continue to show you the same disrespect you show yourself.

LETTING PEOPLE KNOW WHEN THEY HAVE OVERSTEPPED THEIR BOUNDS

Nobody has any right whatsoever to harm you physically or emotionally. Nobody has the right to put you down and to say ugly and hurtful things to you. You must set those limits and let people know when they have overstepped their boundaries. As far as I am concerned, putting a person down is an act of ''verbal violence'' that is just as destructive as a physical attack.

You must immediately confront people who damages your self-esteem. You must let them know in no uncertain terms that what they said was hurtful and unacceptable. In *Toxic People,* I discuss several options available to you in handling these ''toxic'' people: from confronting them, to mirroring their negative behavior back to them, to questioning them directly. Regardless of the technique you use, you must never allow their negative comments to hurt you. Your feelings come first and must be handled accordingly.

THE MINUTE YOU SEE THESE PEOPLE, RUN THE OTHER WAY

Even though, as I mention in *Toxic People,* there are thirty different types of toxic terrors—many of which will be toxic to you only depending on your particular makeup—there are a few types that are universally toxic to everyone. You must run the other way whenever you see someone petty, two-faced, judgmental, or anyone who is a perpetual victim. These people are major sources of trouble.

Even though you can handle almost any type of "toxic" person, depending on who they are and what role they play in your life, if you want to feel great about yourself and be your own best friend, you need to keep these people away from you. Use garlic, an amulet, anything to keep these "energy vampires" out of your life for good.

Petty people are stupid people. They are so concerned with the small and insignificant things in life that they usually miss the big picture. The great Chinese philosopher Confucius had a lot to say about petty people.

Two-faced people can never be trusted with anything. They will often gossip about you and even lie. They are wishy-washy and will be loyal only depending on which way the wind is blowing. They usually fawn over you excessively, singing your praises, only to curse you moments later. Confucius also warns against dangerous people who "befriend someone while concealing a grudge." They are fueled by envy—and envy seeks to destroy. Therefore, they are usually out to destroy you. They do this by sabotaging you and your efforts at every turn. These people are scary because they harbor so much hidden animosity toward you, and you won't know it until you make one comment they don't like, and then they explode like a bomb. (Before they explode, they usually give you a hint that they aren't too crazy about you by peppering their comments with sarcasm, backhanded compliments, and cutting remarks.)

Finally, you will be dragged down to the lowest depths of despair only if you associate with people who are "Gloom and Doom Victims." You can never win with them. You will always feel down around them, as though your energy has been zapped. Heaven forbid you should feel good—much less show that you feel good around them. They will be sure to rain all over your parade. Here is where the old adage "You lie down with dogs, you get fleas" clearly applies. If you associate with Gloom and Doom Victims, their constant problems are bound to rub off on you.

Do yourself the biggest favor ever and never allow any of these "toxic" people into your life, under any circumstances.

If, unfortunately, you have one who is a family member, you may be better off unplugging them from your life for good. In doing so, you will be quite surprised to see how much less stress there is in your life and how your life begins to soar with happiness and positivity.

There are times when we may possess these "toxic traits." After all, we are not perfect 100 percent of the time. The key is to monitor ourselves whenever we exhibit these behaviors. If we consistently demonstrate any of these particular toxic traits, it is in our best interest to seek a qualified therapist to help work out the demons. Otherwise, one will never be able to attract the right friends and influence terrific people to enhance the quality of our lives.

DEALING WITH THE PAIN OF REJECTION WITHOUT SELF-DESTRUCTING

There is nothing more frustrating, more emotionally draining, more humiliating, and more painful than to deal with being rejected. No matter what anyone tells you, it hurts badly. Nobody wants to be rejected, dismissed, or eliminated. No one wants to feel irrelevant or unimportant to someone's life. We all hate it and, unfortunately, we all have to deal with it. The problem is that most of us turn the rejection inward. When we are rejected, we tend to regress to the source of all of our insecurities and to wallow in our pain. Unfortunately, all too often, too many of us stay in this dark, insecure, and self-destructive place. We try to allay the pain in myriad numbing ways: drugs, alcohol, overeating, sleeping too much, not taking care of our health or our personal hygiene, smoking cigarettes, promiscuous sex, and even procrastination.

There are things you can do to help you put rejection into perspective, so that you don't end up slitting your wrists or jumping off a bridge. Here are some healthy things you can do to regain your sanity and your self-worth:

Ways to Put Your Rejection into Perspective

1. Realize that "no" may be "no for now."

2. As difficult as it may be, try to see things from their perspective.

3. Share your emotional reactions to your rejection with others who are your fans, your cheerleaders, and your confidants.

4. See if you can learn something from the alleged reason for your rejection. And, if it's not too stupid a reason, then you may want to make some changes in your life.

5. Ditch your vices. Don't take the rejection out on yourself. You are worth much more than that. Doing negative things to yourself isn't going to hurt anyone else but you, and the few seconds of pleasure are definitely not worth the long-term problems.

6. People are always saying wonderful things to us, but too often we dismiss them, hearing only the bad, the nasty, and the rejecting comments. When people compliment us, we need not dismiss them with perfunctory thanks. Instead, we need to cherish and hear their beautiful words, and carry them with us for the rest of the day— hopefully, for the rest of our lives. Think back to those special words and lovely comments people have made to you, and write them down in your personal "fix your negative traits" notebook that you keep with you at all times. In addition, the next time people compliment you, jot it down in your notebook until you have collected numerous "verbal bouquets"—and they won't lose their sweetness, freshness, and "fragrance" over time. This great self-esteem builder is guaranteed to put you in better spirits, especially if you have met with recent rejection.

In addition, keep a file of fan letters. Save cards announcing your achievements, ones that declare how wonderful people think you are. Whenever you feel down, read and reread them. This uplifting exercise works. I know because I do it often; it helps me to have an even greater appreciation of the work I do to help people.

7. If you are ever in a bad mood and want to feel better immediately, think of all the people whom you know who make you laugh or smile, or the mere thought of whom warms your heart. You may also want to collect photos of these people and keep them in your wallet. Take them out and look at them regularly just to get a positive fix. I do this exercise all the time. It works wonderfully.

8. Substitute vices with wonderful things to pamper yourself. Treat yourself like the prince or princess you always dreamed of being. Don't diminish this—it really works. Each day do whatever you can to better yourself in terms of your outer image and your inner image. Take care of, pamper, and indulge the most important person in the world—*you*. The better you feel, the more tenderly and lovingly you will treat yourself. As others see how well you treat yourself, they will follow suit and give you the same respect you give yourself.

Here is a list to check off each day in order to make sure these areas of your physical self are examined closely, pampered, and attended to.

Pampering Your Outer Image and Self

1. Always be conscious of your personal hygiene—your scent, etc. Use the finest fragrances and pamper yourself on a daily basis with great smelling shampoos, shower and bath products.

2. Pay meticulous attention to your dental hygiene and take care of any dental needs by consulting a dentist immediately.

3. Always make sure your nails are well kept, your hands are smooth and most of all, clean. Whether you are male or female, get regular manicures.

4. Pay close attention to your complexion. Look for areas of roughness and spots. Use lotions and apply necessary medications to assure healthy skin. Always wear sunscreen to prevent skin damage and melanoma that can be deadly.

5. Clean out your ears regularly by making an appointment with an ear, nose, and throat specialist to get wax out so that you can hear better, or use a holistic candling technique that really works wonders in term of aural hygiene.

6. Attend to any medical needs and get annual physical check ups. Don't delay seeing a doctor when anything unusual happens physically. The sooner you get help the more likely you are to repair the damage.

7. In this day and age, if you don't like how you look physically there is no reason to suffer. There are so many things you can do to improve yourself and in turn feel better about yourself, which will give you much more self confidence. Therefore you must attend to your cosmetic needs regularly. This involves your consideration of weight control, makeup, and hair care.

8. Eat well but don't deprive yourself. If you crave something—eat it, just don't go overboard. Life is too short
not to enjoy the pleasures it has to offer and that in-
cludes food.

9. Drink water. You need fluids to keep healthy.

10. Sleep whenever you need it. If you can't sleep, take
advantage of that time you are up and write someone
a note about how much you appreciate them in your
life or how Terrific you think they are. Don't get angry at yourself because you can't sleep. Instead pamper yourself with warm tea and cookies and a good
magazine or book or television until you fall asleep.
One of the reasons why people feel irritable and un-
productive during the day is because they are over-
tired and need a nap. Cranky little kids soon become
uncranky after they are rested so what makes us think
that we adults don't react similarly? Even though it
may not be practical to do so, instead of drinking coffee on your lunch break, go to your car and take a
nap break. A lot of people get the rest they need during the day by taking a twenty minute meditation
break. Afterwards they feel refreshed as though they
slept for hours and are ready to go. They find that
they have more stamina and greater alertness following this short but critical break.

11. You don't have to be an Olympic athlete. Just do some
form of daily exercise to stay fit. Keep moving—even
if it's just a short walk around the block, climbing a
few flights of stairs, or a little work in your garden or
yard.

Pampering Your Inner Image and Self

Equally as important as pampering your outer self is caring for
your inner self. Pay close attention to these guidelines. Try to
follow them religiously.

1. Unload emotional baggage in a therapist's office or with your most intimate friends. Don't moan and groan to everybody around you. They may not want to hear it, and it only makes you look bad.

2. Get rid of any "hatred" within you because "hate consumes the hater." Give it up. Let it go. That is the real meaning of forgiveness.

3. Let go of grudges. Things that are over and done with are over, so don't rehash hard feelings. Know in your heart that "what goes around, comes around."

4. Smile to yourself for no reason at all. Sometimes a smile travels from the face to the soul. It's a form of "*ex-visioning*"—bringing happiness from the outside to within.

5. Never be greedy! Remember that pigs get fat, but hogs get slaughtered. Take what is yours, but don't get carried away.

6. Push to get ahead, but don't shove.

7. Learn something you have always wanted to learn, whether it be a new language, a new sport, or playing an instrument.

8. Read, read, read! Also, learn one new thing each day.

9. Clean your closets. A clean, organized closet often reflects a clear, organized mind. Take control of your closets, your house, your desk, your office, and your car. More control over your environment leads to more control over your life.

10. Redecorate your home or a room in your home. It symbolizes starting over in a fresh new environment and will make you feel as if you have a new lease on life or even a new lease on your home. Sometimes just moving one piece of furniture may give you a feeling of ''newness'' and add to your creativity.

11. Make conscious and conscientious decisions. Many people find it difficult to make accurate decisions. They may be worried about saying no or hurting another person's feelings. Often, they end up hurting themselves by making the wrong decision because they have looked to others for approval of each move they make. It is essential to look at every angle and to analyze every side before you come to a conclusion. Realize that you know what is right for you and what is in your best interest. So do it—and stick to it.

12. Take regular time to do absolutely nothing. Research shows that this downtime reduces stress. Just as a nap or sleep can reenergize you, so can mindless activities. So hug your dog or cat, take a walk, call a friend, organize files, or arrange your sock drawer. You become twice as productive and clearer in your thinking when you take this time for yourself. Be mindful of mindlessness—it's important.

13. Develop your spiritual side. I wouldn't dare dream of telling you how to believe, how to pray, or what religion to follow. I find that people who have a spiritual life have been shown to be a lot happier and to have a greater sense of inner peace than people who don't. If you were born into a religion belief system, you may want to go back to your roots and reexplore those teachings. You will often find that now that you are older, you may gain a better appreciation of it. On the other hand, if it doesn't suit you, you may want to explore other belief systems and other ways of spiritual growth and development. No matter what you believe or how you worship, inner peace comes when you have some type of faith upon which you can call when times may seem bleakest.

THROW AWAY YOUR BURDENS AND
COUNT YOUR BLESSINGS

One of my favorite songs, written by Shelly Peiken and Jeff Bernstein, from My Cat Sushi/Sound Choice is "Count My Blessings." The song literally sends chills through my spine, especially when I hear the incredible harmonies of the four powerful members of the Nylons of Canada, rockapella group. Here are some of their lyrics from their *Rockapella* album which certainly help you to put things into perspective:

In and out of situations
I take the good with the bad
Ups and downs get complicated.
But I don't have to be sad

How about the children who are hungry
And never get to eat
How about the people who are homeless living in the
     street,
        (Refrain)

Every night before I go to sleep
I count my blessings instead of sheep
I say a prayer my soul to keep
I count my blessings.

When I hear the sound of complaining.
I put my hands to my ears.
Think of those whose lives hve been taken
And thank the Lord I am here.

I got some money in my pocket
A hand I can hold.
Somebody standing by me
When winter gets too cold.
     (Refrain)

Things suddenly take on an entirely different perspective when we look at what we do have and appreciate every bit of it, as opposed to lamenting what we don't have.

In order to put our troubles into perspective, we must always remember the old story of the man who was so sad because he didn't have any shoes until he glanced at the man next to him who had no feet.

Remember to count your blessings daily. Here's an exercise I do, and counsel my patients to do whenever a blue funk or negative thought crops up:

"Count Your Blessings" Exercise

1. Write down your specific problem.

2. Directly under it, write down what would be an even worse problem.

3. Now, return to your original problem and, pretending that you are someone's best friend, parent, mentor, or counselor, write down the ideal remedy to the problem.

4. Next, write down every possible step you can take in order to solve this problem. No matter how far-fetched or ridiculous an idea may seem to you, write it down. Do not edit or censor your thoughts.

5. Now go for it. Solve your problem in an intelligent and systematic way. Follow the best solutions you listed in Step 4. Take the risk. Take the chance. Just make sure you don't hurt anyone in solving your problem. Otherwise, anything goes.

6. Next, list every single blessing you have. List the terrific people who have graced your life in the past, and who are in your life today. List what you have: your education, your family. Keep this list with you at all times, adding to it along the way. Add even the simplest blessings. For example, let's say you went to the doctor to cure your cold, and he gave you the medication that cured you. Write it down, and appreciate all the good things that came to you.

7. Look at this list for inspiration whenever you are feeling blue, or when you just want a mental pick-me-up.

ACCEPT THE HELP—YOU DESERVE IT

People feel that they are either too proud, that they don't want to impose, or that they can do it themselves. The truth is that they have such poor feelings of self-worth that they don't feel that they deserve the help. As any successful businessperson will tell you, the key to success and ultimate happiness is taking advantage of every opportunity that comes your way. Opportunities come in many forms, and you must accept offers of help from others graciously and walk through the doors other people are willing to open for you. If you are not proactive when it comes to calling and following up on a reference or a contact you were given, or if you do not go out of your way to nurture certain potential terrific relationships, you have taken their million-dollar gift and thrown it into the garbage.

When you start to feel good about yourself, you will begin to feel worthy and entitled to receiving terrific actions from others in your life.

Because they are following your lead, people will want to do more to help you enhance whatever aspects in your life that they can. Since they have observed your standards of positive self-enhancing behavior, they will usually treat you with the same respect you have given yourself.

Becoming That Terrific Person to Others

*H*ave you ever noticed that there are people whom everyone seems to love and adore? Few people don't take to them, or don't have kind things to say about them. These popular people have few enemies, if any, and seem to get along with just about everyone they come in contact with. Indeed, "to know them is to love them."

Talk-show personality Leeza Gibbons is one of these terrific people. Along with everyone else who knows Leeza, I love her. She is as beautiful on the inside as she is on the outside. Everyone she comes in contact with—from her staff to her guests, from the press to the public—will tell you the same thing. They love Leeza.

Why? Because Leeza is real. She is not a hypocrite. She is honest and trustworthy. She never exploits people. In the days when television talk shows did whatever it took to assure blockbuster ratings, Leeza, like Oprah Winfrey, never sold out. Both of these women always maintained their decency, integrity, and humanity by continuing to take the high road even when it wasn't the popular thing to do.

What makes people like Leeza and Oprah so terrific is that these extraordinary people clearly know how to be terrific to others. The more terrifically you treat others, the more terrific you become. Virtually every major religion holds to this philosophy and shares this universal truth: What you give you will receive.

RECIPROCITY IS THE KEY TO BEING A TERRIFIC PERSON

Whether it is as the Old Testament says, "casting your bread upon the waters and having it return to you," or as the New Testament says, "reaping what you sow," or the Hindu philosophy of "enkarma"—doing good for others and having it return to you, the Buddhist philosophy of "cause and effect," or even the old Japanese adage, "When you do for others, the gods will repay you," there is surely a reciprocal relationship between giving and getting.

Most of us are not manipulative and don't give in order to get. We give for the sake of giving. And through this act, we end up receiving. Perhaps the old Chinese saying sums it up best; when we give someone a rose, the scent of the rose also lingers on our hand.

This example of the rose clearly illustrates the concept of reciprocity. Toddlers know this concept better than anyone else when they go through the stage of development from nine to twelve months of age where they give you things. Whether they place their favorite toy or a chewed-up piece of cookie into your hand, they delight with your delight that they gave you something. The more pleased they see you are, the more they repeat this action of giving. They like the fact that they did something that caused you to react positively toward them, which in turn makes them feel good and want to repeat that behavior. When you, in turn, reciprocate by giving something back to them (such as a toy), they too, smile, and verbalize their delight with an array of happy noises, coos, and squeals and by showing you the ultimate sign of their appreciation—placing your "gift" in their mouth.

Your appreciation of their action encourages them to give more, just as their appreciation of your action makes you want to give more. This mutual act of giving and receiving is what all terrific relationships are based on.

Giving to one another is a two-way street. When relationships are one-sided, where only one of the parties is the giver and the other takes and doesn't give back, or doesn't give back in the same manner, then the relationship ceases to be terrific. Hard feelings and conflict usually arise out of a relationship that is not mutually reciprocal. Whether it is a business relationship, friendship, or marriage, if there is not reciprocity, the relationship will definitely suffer and eventually come to an end because inevitably hard feelings will surface.

No human being wants to feel used or taken advantage of. The frustration of doing and doing and doing and not getting anything in return often turns to self-destructive behavior, or even to overt anger. Look at what happens with the simple act of putting money into a vending machine. When you don't get what you paid for, you push the button again. Then you push the coin return, and when nothing comes out, you may even slam the machine. You are angry and have every right to be. It is human nature to become angry and frustrated when you don't get something you paid for.

The same is true for human interaction. You must give and get something back from the people to whom you gave something. Whether you gave them something material, intellectual, or emotional, you need to receive from them in return. Otherwise, you will not feel satisfied. Look what happens even in conversation. Let's say you meet people and talk to them about your interests and share your beliefs. Are you going to want to continue talking to them if they don't reciprocate in the conversation and share something about themselves? Of course not. Otherwise you might as well be talking to a tree. Conversation is not a monologue; it is a dialogue where there is a mutual give-and-take in the conversation. When you say something that stimulates him and he says something that stimulates you, the two of you can talk for hours and hours.

You can rationalize all you want by thinking that even though you give to someone and receive nothing in return, it's all right and that you will be receiving from other sources. The reality is that it is *not* all right. It does not erase the emotional slap in the face you feel when someone to whom you are generous doesn't give back. Let's face it—it may hurt your feelings deeply. When you have finally experienced enough hurt and pain to ''unplug'' and walk away, you will feel a sense of relief because you have regained your self-worth and self-respect.

Michelle treated Roger like a king. She gave all she had. She was physically affectionate to him and never refused his sexual advances, gave him endless massages, made him great meals, bought him numerous gifts that she thought he would need and like, and went wherever he wanted to go—even on fishing trips, sporting events, and action movies of which she was not very fond. She was always there for him.

Unfortunately, her generosity and caring weren't reciprocated. After two years of his lack of attention, Michelle got so fed up that she walked away and never looked back. She wasn't even sad. In fact, she was thrilled. She gave and gave and got nothing except frustration, which turned into anger, then to hurt. When she left him, she left the pain behind as well.

Bill Farley, President and CEO of Farley Industries, which owns Fruit of the Loom and many other businesses, believes that the reason for his enormous success in life is not only due to being blessed with a great family who supported and encouraged him all the way, but to a wonderful well-rounded education that gave him the tools and the confidence to accomplish all of the remarkable things he has done throughout his life. To show his appreciation, he recently not only made a seven-figure gift to his high school in Rhode Island and started a scholarship program for deserving young students, but he also gave students the special gift of his inspiring words in an emotionally moving speech that touched the hearts of everyone who heard it. Year after year, he continues to show his appreciation for his excellent college education at Bowdoin College by donating significant amounts of money so that the school can not only have better athletic facilities, but a state-of-the-art science program as well.

When Good Things Happen to Good People

Bill Farley has it all. He is extremely wealthy. He has a yacht, a private plane, and gorgeous homes all over the country. He travels around the world and can afford to buy whatever he wants. He has a lovely, accomplished, talented, and stunningly beautiful wife and a spectacular three-year-old son, Liam, who is the apple of his eye. Bill Farley is also extremely brilliant. He has movie-star good looks, and a healthy and athletic body that belies his age by twenty years. He has a very upbeat and effervescent personality combined with a positive winning attitude toward life. To top it off, Bill is caring, sensitive, and generous.

Many people would be jealous or envious of Bill's life. They would credit his success to luck or wealthy parents or marrying into the right family. But these people don't know how Bill Farley got to be one of the most terrific people in the world. They would have no clue that he came from humble beginnings. His father was a postal worker and his mother a housewife. He put himself through college doing all sorts of menial jobs in order to earn enough money. He also put himself through law school, where his hard work ended up getting him a job at a prestigious law firm on Wall Street.

He had the courage to follow his dream and took a risk by changing professions and entering the field of finance. He continued to take even bigger risks and live out his dreams until he became one of the youngest people in the nation to purchase a major company, Fruit of the Loom. He continued to follow his dreams and acquire numerous other companies and build them up to be enormously profitable, thereby creating Farley Industries.

Bill became so successful by knowing the value of meeting people through people and surrounding himself only with other successful people who were the best in their particular businesses, learning from them, and networking with them.

Bill is so generous and appreciative of whatever he has that he has given back to so many—not only to his schools, but to his family and friends. He has helped many needy individuals, supported countless charities, and helped many others get back on their feet when they were down and out, with both financial and moral support. He has generously made contacts and opened doors for many people which, in turn, has turned their lives around and afforded them opportunities that they never would have had before.

Bill Farley and other highly accomplished and terrific people like him have worked extremely hard to get where they are, and they deserve all the good that life has to offer them. They have more because they take more chances, and they take advantage of more opportunities. We need to substitute any feelings of jealousy or envy toward them with feelings of hope and inspiration. We need to uplift these people and hold them up as role models who empower us, and who lead us in the direction of finding our own "terrificness."

ARE YOU A TERRIFIC PERSON TO SOMEONE?

If we asked most people if they thought they were terrific to others, most would agree that they are. However, if we asked those to whom they thought they were supposedly being terrific, we might often find that we would get a different opinion. Being terrific means that you are giving, generous, helpful, caring, sensitive, kind, and empowering consistently.

THE TEN GUIDELINES TO BEING TERRIFIC TO OTHERS

Here are ten guidelines that you need to follow religiously to assure that you are being a terrific person to others:

1. Treat the Ones You Love Better Than Anyone Else in the World

Instead of taking for granted those with whom you are most familiar, pay them the most attention. You need to cherish and nurture them and think about them as much—if not more—than you think of yourself. You need to constantly be on the alert for ways to improve their lives, ways to please them, and ways to make them happy. Go out of your way to do things you are sure they want and love—not what you want or think they would want.

For example, let's say you are passing a gift shop and notice a cobalt blue pen in the window. You know that cobalt blue is your friend's favorite color, and you also know that she loves pens. Stop what you are doing and go out of your way to surprise her with this thoughtful gift.

A client of mine knew that his girlfriend loved the perfume from the spa at the Parc Monceau Hotel in Paris. The perfume wasn't available anywhere else in the world. He made special arrangements to have several bottles shipped to her directly; it wasn't her birthday or any holiday, he just wanted to show her that he cared about her enough to go out of his way to find the perfume and have it shipped from Paris. It helped to cement their relationship and make them even closer.

I know many women who have received marriage proposals from their husbands after they went out of their way to do something spectacular for them. My friend Sandra truly wanted to marry Jerry. Although he loved her, he had cold feet because of a previous awful marriage and many unhappy relationships. For his fiftieth birthday, she threw him a surprise bash, inviting friends he hadn't seen in years. Because he was an avid sailor, she rented a yacht for the evening, along with a tuxedo for him to change into when he unknowingly arrived on board. The gifts he received were spectacular, including the jet ski that Sandra had all of his friends pitch in to pay for. However, Jerry's favorite gift was the one orchestrated by Sandra, which he received when they got home. She had arranged for five beautiful women to give him a makeover: manicure, pedicure, haircut, facial, and massage. Afterward, Sandra ran him a sensual bath, complete with foam, rose petals, scented oil, and candles. She poured him champagne and fed him caviar and strawberries dipped in white chocolate. Then, she dried him off sensually with the brand-new luscious bath towel she'd bought him, led him by the hand to the bed, which she made up with brand-new soft Egyptian cotton sheets, and made passionate love to him. Needless to say, Jerry was overwhelmed by this wonderful treatment. He figured that if she went out of her way to do this for him, she must truly love him. He asked her to marry him when the sun came up the next morning.

Pamper the people you love constantly. Cherish them and indulge them at all times, thereby making them feel as though they are the most important person in the world—especially your world. Kiss them the way they want to be kissed, hold them the way they want to be held, and love them as they want to be loved. Speak to them the way they want to be spoken to. By respecting their needs and putting them first, you can't help seeing things from their viewpoint. The more you do for them, the more they will cherish and appreciate you, and the more they will do for you.

2. Consistently Speak Lovingly to Them and About Them

Mother Theresa once said, "Kind words are simple, but their echoes are endless." When we speak kindly to another person, with gentle, soft loving tones, we let them know that we truly like them. When we first hear their voices, they know that we are thrilled to hear from them because of the upbeat bounce in our voice. We need to tell them openly and freely how much we adore them and how much we appreciate them in our lives. This way they are reassured of our love.

If you have to tell them something that is a bit unpleasant, do it in a way that does not make them feel judged or talked down to. Instead, assure them that you love them, that you are on their side, and see things from their point of view, and trust their judgment. But you would like to offer them another point of view to consider. Always keep in mind that it is not just what you say but how you say it that counts. Even though you must always be honest, diplomacy is a priority.

Sing their praises consistently, not only to them directly, but to others. You must be the best public-relations agent they can ever have. You need to always be on the lookout for people who could help them, projects they can get involved with, or anything else that could improve the quality of their life.

Consuela always goes to parties with her husband, the CEO of a major company, and constantly keeps her friends Rebecca, Greta, and Pat in mind. She keeps an eye out for an eligible bachelor for her single friend, Rebecca. Greta is a free-lance writer, so Consuela looks for people in the publishing or literary world with whom to connect Greta. And she tells anyone who compliments her on one of the exotic outfits she usually wears about her friend Pat, who designed them. Consuela's selfless public-relations efforts have paid off. Rebecca now has a fiancé, Greta now has a literary agent, and Pat's business has tripled as a result of Consuela's efforts at promotion.

3. Never Take Your Anxieties or Troubles out on Others

Just because you are having a bad day, don't take it out on someone else. If you are angry at Iris, stay angry at Iris. Don't transfer your anger onto Jacqueline. Don't bring your anger to anyone other than the person who made you angry or who upset you. Doing otherwise is unconscionable and makes you toxic.

Acknowledge the actual source of your anger by taking a deeper look into your life and examining whom you are truly angry with. Refrain from projecting that anger onto others. Not all men are jerks just because you have had a string of bad relationships. If you had trouble getting along with your mother, you have to realize consciously that not all women are your mother.

In addition, don't vent all over other people. Sometimes people will call you up or you will call them just to vent about another person. When finished ranting and raving, you—or they—usually feel a great sense of relief. However, it is a different story with the person to whom you or they were just ranting and raving. They now feel as though they have been run over emotionally by a bulldozer after being lashed out at, when they had absolutely nothing to do with the situation or problem. That is not how terrific people treat their close friends. Instead, they address and settle their problems with the person who caused the trouble.

4. Being a Terrific Person Means Having to Say You're Sorry—and Meaning It

Everyone in the world makes mistakes—even terrific people. However, they are quick to admit their errors and apologize readily and sincerely for their transgressions. They make every attempt to rectify the situation, and they usually don't make the same mistake twice. They know the value of saying "I am sorry" and how much it means to that person's self-esteem to be treated respectfully. In the 1970s, many people believed the slogan made popular by the movie *Love Story*. "Love is never having to say you are sorry." On the contrary, love is not only having to *say* you are sorry, but to really mean it.

When the world seemed to be crashing down on Twyla, she inappropriately took out her frustrations on her twelve-year-old son, Todd, by accusing him of taking a one-hundred-dollar bill that was lying on the coffee table. He had no clue what she was talking about; he had never seen the money, let alone thought to steal it. She wouldn't let him explain, called him a "little thief," and threatened to have him put in juvenile hall. Todd was stunned to see his mother so out of control. She was ready to hit him, something she had never done before. She barged into his room, removed his television and video games, ordered him to stay in his room, grounded him from seeing his friends and playing soccer the next day, and canceled his weekend camping trip with the Boy Scouts. He was so humiliated and frustrated that for the first time, he had thoughts of running away from home.

Twyla found the money a half-hour later, in an envelope in which she had placed it, but forgotten about. She felt horrible about accusing Todd and came into his room immediately with tears in her eyes.

She apologized profusely for accusing him and for even thinking that he would do something like that. She hugged him and held him and, as she cried, told him why she was feeling so overwhelmed—the threat of being laid off from her job, her mother's poor health and all of the medical expenses that went with it, and her present financial concerns.

Todd clearly understood and told his mother that he fully appreciated her being so open with him by telling him she was sorry and admitting that she was wrong. He even offered to help out by trying to earn some extra money by mowing lawns, delivering papers, or taking care of the twins across the street. Needless to say, Twyla was deeply moved. Her readily admitting that she was wrong and discussing what her anger was really about opened the lines of communication between them.

5. Give, Give, and Give Some More—Then Go That Extra Mile

It's not just enough to give when it is convenient for you. It is even more important to give when giving is difficult or challenging for you. Many charities and churches talk about ''giving until it hurts.''

This type of giving is what happens when you offer to take care of someone's children so that they can go out and enjoy themselves, when you would rather be out as well. It involves helping a coworker finish a proposal when you would rather be working on your own projects or going home for the day.

It involves taking the time to put your needs and concerns on hold while you help others make their lives a little better. Then and only then can you honestly say that you went that extra mile. Look at Lewis Trujillo, a sixty-four-year-old Colorado man. After he saw a television show about the plight of Native American children, he was so moved that he sold his truck and used the money to buy nearly 70,000 pounds of used clothing for them. He then shipped this clothing to the most poverty-stricken Indian reservations.

Today his Night Walker Enterprises has collected, shipped, and distributed over 3 million pounds of food, clothing, supplies, and toys to more than 100,000 Native Americans across the country.

Mr. Trujillo gave until his pocketbook was stretched to the limit. His generous venture has put him into debt. However, he is not at all concerned because he believes so strongly that he has made such a significant difference in the lives of others.

Terrific people are immediate in their response to need in others. They are always thinking of ways to assist people whom they meet and know. Nobody has to ask them for help because they volunteer their assistance immediately.

6. Give Up Looking at Differences and Finger-Pointing—Instead, Look for Similarities

When we see the similarities in others, we feel close to them. When we see their differences, all we feel is distance and alienation. After dissecting cadavers during my medical training, working with enough of the most severely deformed and physically challenged people, working with the rich, famous, beautiful, and accomplished people in the world, I have come to the conclusion that all human beings on this earth, no matter what shape or form, are more like one another than they are different from one another. Everyone bleeds, perspires, coughs, burps, passes gas, urinates, and defecates. All people long to feel important, to be loved and appreciated, and to reciprocate those same feelings. It doesn't matter how we are packaged, how dark or light our skin, we are more alike than we can ever imagine. If we look for that "alikeness," we are guaranteed to have more love in our hearts and less hatred.

To best illustrate this point, I call upon one of my favorite moments in history, when black South African leader Nelson Mandela and white South African leader F. W. de Klerk shared the Nobel Peace Prize. Although they appear so different physically, they are very similar intellectually, emotionally, and morally. Both are brilliant men of the highest integrity and inner strength, and both share the same vision for world peace and harmony.

Terrific people don't spend their energies judging others. Instead, much like the Buddhist philosophy, they acknowledge and accept others for who they are. They don't try to fight other people's natures or belief systems. Even though they may acknowledge that others views may be different from theirs and therefore frustrating, they never lose sight of others' humanity. Their views may be different, but their basic needs are the same as ours.

7. *When Good Things Happen to Others, Get as Excited as If They Had Happened to You*

When you experience another person's joy as though it were your own, you have definitely evolved as a terrific person. When you are not jealous or petty and have true empathy, you can unselfishly feel excitement for others. When you want the best for others and see something good happening for them, you are uplifted and inspired by their good fortune.

When Theresa found out that Niki was getting married, she was ecstatic. As she listened to the news over the telephone one morning, her screams of joy nearly woke up the entire neighborhood. She loved Niki very much and knew how much marrying Thomas meant to her.

At Niki's wedding, Theresa was so nervous that she felt like a bride herself. Because of her great compassion and empathy for Niki, the two friends were able to form an even closer bond. Niki sincerely felt Theresa's good wishes and love, which made her reciprocate those feelings to Theresa.

When Josh came into his colleague's office with a huge grin indicating that he got the promotion that Dick also wanted, Dick was truly happy for him. He jumped up, slapped Josh on the back, gave him a smile, and said, "Hey, bud, let's get out of here and celebrate! Lunch is on me, and I'll even buy you a drink!" There was such a great camaraderie between these two men that neither one was threatened by the other. Sure, Dick would have loved to have gotten the promotion, but Josh's getting it was good enough. Dick was confident in his abilities and knew that he was liked in the company. He knew that it was only a matter of time until he, too, climbed up the corporate ladder. In fact, it came to pass quickly, as Josh was now in a position to help him get a promotion and a raise— which he did.

8. Don't Sweat the Small Stuff—Never Be Petty

Never play "tit for tat" or "I did this and you didn't do that" with anyone. Instead, do things because you want to do things to help others, not because there is something in it for you. It goes without saying that the person for whom you chose to do something for will be appreciative and will reciprocate in some way, but it is nothing that you should expect, demand, or depend on.

If you want to be a terrific person, there is no room for pettiness. Terrific people are never small-minded or petty. Instead, they are magnanimous, generous, and see the bigger picture, not the minutiae. Terrific people don't keep score, and when they surround themselves with other terrific people, everything ends up balancing out.

Beverly's pettiness drove all potential terrific relationships— both male and female—out of her life within a short time of anyone knowing her. Whenever she went to lunch or dinner with a friend and they split the bill, she would total up her portion to the exact penny.

She was so concerned about every nickel and dime that when someone invited her to a concert, the first thing she asked was how much it cost, and would she have to pay because they were inviting her. Her whole life was consumed with getting deals and asking for freebies that after spending a few hours with her, any self-respecting person would be turned off. They found her petty behavior to be so embarrassing that they generally never got together with her again.

Terrific people simply don't think or behave like this, and they have no room for people who do.

9. Empower and Inspire Others by Believing in Them

Terrific people not only give people a "fish" to eat, they also provide them with the "fishing pole," so that they can catch the fish for themselves, and have food all the time. This old Chinese proverb reflects how we must give in order to empower people.

Perhaps nobody knows this better than Dr. Mimi Silbert, a recognized expert in criminal psychology, who founded Delancey Street. This organization provides criminal offenders, ex-felons, homeless, and drug addicts with the tools to take responsibility—both good and bad.

Fueled by her belief that everyone wants to be somebody, and that everyone is both a giver and a receiver, she has rescued over 11,000 people by teaching them the skills to become productive members of society. In essence, everyone gets training in one form of physical labor, one service job, and one "desk" job. Then each individual concentrates in one of these three areas and learns as much as possible in order to have sufficient skills to do the job. Everyone who is a resident at the facility tutors and teaches other residents. They have frequent outings to museums and musical performances regularly, so they learn new things all the time. Twice a week they go to group sessions to learn how to communicate and handle their emotional difficulties. By teaching people new skills, giving them new opportunities, and giving them the knowledge that it is up to them to take responsibility for who they are today, Dr. Silbert provides them with valuable tools of empowerment. These tools allow them to catch the biggest, tastiest, and most life-sustaining "fish" for the rest of their lives.

Sometimes terrific people don't have to do anything to empower another person, except to just "be there." Just your presence alone may encourage others to be the best they can be. Be there for others, and they'll be there for you.

10. Always Perpetuate the Spiral of Friendship— Share Other Terrific People

I can't state frequently enough that if you meet people who may be of value or helpful to another person—pass them on! Don't just think of yourself and what you can get out of the situation and the relationship. Instead, always think of other people and what and who might be helpful to them.

When you see that someone whom you know might benefit in some way from knowing another person, you are creating the best of goodwill by introducing them to each other.

Chapter 7

When Terrific People Disappoint You

- *Dealing with Disillusionment*
- *What Causes Terrific People to Turn Toxic?*
- *The One-Two-Three Test*
- *Ending the Once-Terrific Relationship*
- *Recovering When Terrific Relationships End*
- *Rekindling a Former Terrific Relationship That Once Turned Sour*

*E*ven though a person may be terrific, they may still end up disappointing you. Terrific people are not perfect, and their wonderful qualities do not make them immune to the frailties of being human.

Sometimes people are insensitive and self-consumed. They may not be there for you when you really need them; they may lose their temper, or even make a scene in public. They may procrastinate about doing something that they promised to do for you, or not do it at all. They may be curt or impatient with you. They may even be judgmental, surprising you with a negative comment about yourself. Instead of being supportive and sensitive, they may even react harshly and angrily to a precarious situation into which you may have gotten yourself.

Even though these behaviors seem out of character for them and may shock you, you have to always keep in mind that although they are "super" human beings, they are not "superhuman" beings. They are not God, and they are not saints. And perhaps the reason they behave badly may lie in what is going on in their own lives.

Jack and Jeanie were the best of friends. During the past five years, they told each other everything. Jack was the helpful and supportive "big brother" Jeanie had always wanted, and Jeanie was the perky and cute "little sister" that Jack had always wanted. One day Jeanie was discussing a boyfriend problem with Jack and was shocked to hear the following words spew from his mouth; "Why don't you grow up and stop acting like a child? Handle it and act like an adult, and stop playing that cutesy game with everyone. This way, you'll stop getting into these situations in the first place."

After regaining her composure, Jeanie vowed never to speak to him again. Jack felt bad about his action and apologized profusely to Jeanie the next day. He then explained how much he loved her as a friend, and how he hated to see her in so much pain as the result of being with men who were unworthy of her. Because Jack explained his position so well, and because this was a one-time negative action in the five years they had been friends, Jeanie forgave him readily. Their friendship was back on track.

Had Jack continued to speak to Jeanie in that judgmental and condescending manner, then there would have been a big problem, and Jeanie would not have continued their friendship. The good news is that terrific people do not display nasty behavior or make disrespectful comments to you consistently. If they do, then they have turned toxic with you.

DEALING WITH DISILLUSIONMENT

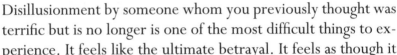

Disillusionment by someone whom you previously thought was terrific but is no longer is one of the most difficult things to experience. It feels like the ultimate betrayal. It feels as though it is not the same person you once knew, and you have no clue as to what happened to change him or her. It is devastatingly sad, and the grief makes you feel as if a death has taken place. In actuality, there has been a death—a death of the relationship.

When a terrific person disappoints them, the first thing people usually do is blame themselves and doubt their own judgment. They think, "How could I have ever trusted this person or thought that this person was wonderful? How could I think that she was terrific? What's wrong with me that I couldn't see through him or read his signs properly?"

In reality, you may have been reading those signs properly all along. Those people just may not have presented their negative behaviors to you. Therefore, there is no way you would have known—or you very well might have read them correctly all along because they were indeed terrific to you—at one time. They just turned "un-terrific."

The keys in dealing with the disillusionment is not to doubt or blame yourself, and not to go overboard and end up detesting the other person. When you feel betrayed or question your own judgment, it is a common psychological reaction to feel intense dislike—if not hatred—toward the other person. The reaction is so strong because the pain and confusion is so deep.

WHAT CAUSES TERRIFIC PEOPLE TO TURN TOXIC?

There are three main reasons why people turn toxic: they are jealous, feel inadequate or threatened, or there is some type of miscommunication.

Jealousy and envy are at the root of all evil behaviors, and they destroy. Most often, you see this directed at people in the public eye, who seem to have it all. The press builds them up one minute and tears them down the next. Why? Because of jealousy, envy, and not wanting these superstars to have it all, they write horrible and nasty things about them in the press. How many of us tear another person down verbally because we are envious of them, seeking to destroy them with such comments as "They aren't so great," or "I know such-and-such about them."

Feelings of jealousy are tied closely to those of inadequacy. If you do not feel secure in your own worth, seeing others do well not only threatens your self-esteem, but also adds to your feelings of unworthiness. Symptoms of this in a formerly terrific friend include trying to control you in order to get the upper hand, tearing you down in front of others, and, in general, not being supportive of you.

The third reason why a once-terrific relationship may turn toxic is due to miscommunication, where both parties aren't getting their points across adequately. This was the case with business partners Joseph and Marty. Joseph thought that Marty didn't trust him because he checked and double-checked Joseph's work constantly. This insulted and upset Joseph so much that he lashed out at Marty verbally, and the two almost got into a fistfight. In reality, Marty didn't feel that he was doubting Joseph's honesty at all. He behaved the same way with his own work, and checked, rechecked and triple-checked all of his orders as well. After tempers died down, Marty explained his concerns and shared his true, insecure feelings with Joseph. He told him that since this was the biggest order in the history of their company, he didn't want to do anything to mess things up. And since his last business went bankrupt because he didn't pay fastidious attention to detail, he had made it a point to be very conscientious in this new venture. After their open discussion, Joseph now clearly understood the reason for Marty's neurotic behavior, and he was no longer furious with him.

In turn, Joseph told Marty that he was the type of person who went ballistic if he was watched or monitored. He didn't need a watchdog or a guard standing over him. Now that the two men have opened the channels of communication between them, they have resumed a terrific business relationship and have made lots of money together.

You can forgive and resume the relationship if the reason for your disharmony was the result of a miscommunication, which you were able to resolve. In this case, when people apologize, you know that they truly mean it and that they have your best interests at heart. On the other hand, if the reason for the breakup is due to jealousy, or feelings of insecurity or inadequacy, there is no way that the relationship can, nor should, be repaired or continue.

THE ONE-TWO-THREE TEST

Unfortunately, if respect and communication aren't consistent, the once-terrific relationship will end. It should never end immediately; several attempts at communication should be made before you conclude that the relationship is over. A dear friend of mine, Tracie Hunt Mayer, who is a spiritual counselor to many prominent people, offers her "One-Two-Three" technique, which has been very successful for her clients. When terrific people bring them disappointment, instead of "throwing the baby out with the bathwater" and dismissing them completely, she recommends following these steps:

1. Acknowledge the pain and the hurt, and in a civilized, calm way tell the terrific people that their actions have caused you emotional distress. Often, Step 1 is the only step you need to take. You have communicated your displeasure immediately, and they have initiated action immediately in an attempt to modify and rectify the situation. Because they are so terrific, they are generally more sensitive to your feelings, which will make them more conscious of your displeasure.

   However, if they continue their negative actions and are still insensitive to your requests, Step 2 is necessary.

2. In a firmer and more direct manner, confront them by setting specific limitations and indicate that you will not tolerate their pattern of negative behavior. Let them know there are serious consequences to their behavior. If their behavior persists and your wishes go unheeded, or you are disrespected continually, then you have no other choice than to go to Step 3.

3. In this final step, you leave and don't look back. If these terrific people, who are supposed to be so sensitive to your wants and needs aren't, even after repeated attempts at communication, then there is something else that is underlying their hostile actions toward you. As discussed earlier, that something else may be jealousy, envy, competition, or disrespect for you. In any event, you can no longer afford to have these people in your life.

ENDING THE ONCE-TERRIFIC RELATIONSHIP

For most people, ending a once-terrific relationship is the hardest thing in the world. However, if you remember the lyrics of the old Jim Croce song, "For every time that I spent laughing, there were two times that I cried," you will remind yourself why you had to part ways. Nobody deserves to be disrespected. Nobody deserves to be unhappy and feel miserable more often than they feel good when they are with a loved one.

Although many people end relationships in a heated battle with tempers flaring all over the place, it is better if closure of the relationship takes place in a more civilized and controlled manner. This way both parties can leave with their dignity and self-respect somewhat intact. Depending on your preference, there are several ways you can close the chapter of a bad relationship: through direct verbal communication, writing a letter, by a message on an answering machine, and even by using a third party. You cannot ignore the situation. You cannot walk away and say or do nothing. That isn't fair to you, to the other person, or to the integrity of your once-terrific relationship.

Direct Verbal Communication in Person

Ending a relationship in person is perhaps the most difficult way, but is often the most thorough. You can clearly look at and hear the people and read how they really feel about you. Remember not to be accusatory—that only fuels tempers. Even though it will be a highly emotional experience for you, remember to talk in terms of you and your experiences. Don't say things like "You did this to me and you did that to me." Instead, say, "I am feeling very disturbed about our relationship. I don't feel comfortable with the fact that you said . . ." This way, you are taking full responsibility for your lack of contentment in the relationship, and you are being proactive in taking the necessary steps to terminate the relationship. Allow others to save face, and try to keep your anger in check, so that you don't get into a heated blowup that leaves even more damage than there was before. Be direct. Get to the point, be clear about the issues at hand, and about the result you want to achieve—which is to walk away with dignity.

Sometimes, talking face to face may reignite the once-terrific friendship and get it back on track, especially if it stimulates a more open discussion, where points of view and perspective are laid out clearly and openly.

Writing a Letter and Faxing It

Writing a letter may be the best way to end a relationship because the once-terrific person has the opportunity to examine and reexamine your thoughts and feelings. You also have the opportunity to organize your thoughts and feelings and express them without being interrupted and distracted as you might be in conversation with that person. In writing the letter, do not let your focus get convoluted. Make your important points. Start off with an intention statement, which may read like this:

Dear Amy:

I am writing you this letter because I have been very disturbed by what has happened in our relationship. It is so disturbing to me that I do not wish to continue it for the following reasons . . .

Then list the specific incidents and your reactions to them. For example:

I feel as though I am walking on eggshells whenever I am around you. I experience your harsh tones and tense facial expression whenever you talk to me. I was very disturbed when you practically bit my head off when I asked you the simple question: "What do you think we ought to do about making the calls to all the people who will be attending the event."
I feel as though you disrespect my wishes. Every time I ask you to do something, you ignore me and don't re-

spond, and you never act upon what I suggest. This makes me feel as though I do not matter.

Next, summarize the good points of your relationship; what your friend brought to it that was positive, and what you brought to it that was good. Then state that at this point you cannot continue the relationship in good conscience since it is clearly no longer a positive or pleasant experience for either of you. Wish him or her well, and hope that he or she finds ''inner peace.''

Depending on whether the other person has a private or public fax machine, you may or may not want to fax the letter. In order to assure that the person gets the letter, you may want to have it messengered, sent as E-mail, or sent by express mail.

Leaving a Message on a Telephone-Answering Machine

Sometimes it may be virtually impossible to end the relationship over the phone because tempers may flare and it may be hard to hear what the other person is saying. On the phone, it is often the person who speaks the loudest who gets heard. If your relationship has reached this level, it is too easy to insult each other further by hanging up abruptly. It may be better to call when you don't think the person will be home, and leave the message on the answering machine. Often, answering machines have such little time allotted on the tape that you need to get to the point as soon as possible. If the message time is too short, you may want to call back and leave a series of messages until you say everything that you want to.

RECOVERING WHEN TERRIFIC RELATIONSHIPS END

When a terrific relationship ends you can't help feeling devastated. There is a great sense of loss because you have so many memories of terrific times shared together. You think back to those marvelous moments, and it depresses you all over again. You will go through a grieving process much like grieving over a death. You will go through the stages of denial, in which you may doubt that the negative events really happened. You may ask yourself whether the person really behaved that way, or whether it was just something you exaggerated. This is the stage at which you have to be extremely careful because you are quite vulnerable. It is easy to go back to the now-toxic individual, act as though nothing has happened, and try to resume your once-terrific relationship. The only problem is that you will end up experiencing the same pain and frustration later on, and the cycle will continue all over again.

You may also find yourself going through a major "rage stage," in which you end up hating the person. You want to rip up any card or photo he ever gave you, and either throw away or give away any gift you ever received from her. You want nothing to remind you of your past relationship. You may even find yourself bad-mouthing the person to everyone who knows him or her, and even to those who don't. You will find yourself talking to everyone about how you trusted the person and how he or she did you wrong. You may also find that you will go through full-blown depression, where you can't eat, can't sleep, are forgetful, feel fragmented, and can't concentrate. Here are several things you can do to facilitate the healing process.

1. See a professional counselor for help. You can vent your anger and frustration, and therapy can help you to see what really happened in your relationship a lot more clearly.

2. Take some time off from work and from your social life to regroup and to readjust.

3. Do everything listed in Chapter Five of this book in the sections "Pampering Your Outer Self" and "Pampering Your Inner Self."

4. Meet new people. Even though you may not feel like it, you have to force yourself to get out and about and mingle. Talk to people using the techniques in this book.

5. Whenever you are feeling the hurt and pain, use the "Stop the Thought" technique described in my book *Toxic People*. Take a breath in through your mouth, hold it for a few seconds, and then say to yourself, "Stop the thought." Substitute a more pleasant thought.

6. Never bad-mouth the person because it restimulates your negative feelings. If you continue to rehash the problem, it lives and breathes as though it has just happened Let it go. Besides, once upon a time, you actually cherished that terrific person in your life. You don't have to hate the person because the relationship changed. You just need to move on.

When famed Hollywood producer Don Simpson—who, along with his partner, Jerry Bruckheimer, produced *Top Gun, Flashdance, and Fame*—died, everyone wanted to dig up the dirt and find out what really happened to Don. (He was known to have a drug problem, and myriad emotional problems because he lived life on the edge.) Perhaps the classiest comment I ever heard was made by his partner, Jerry Bruckheimer, in *Vanity Fair*. In response to questions about his late partner's character and behavior, Jerry's simple comment, "I am going to protect him in death as I protected him in life," spoke volumes.

Look to Jerry's comment as an example of how we need to refrain from adding more fuel to any negative commentary about others than already exists. Even though once-terrific people may no longer have roles in your life, the fact that they once did is reason enough not to spew venom. You don't have to hate them just because the relationship is no longer viable. In order to dissipate the anger and hatred, you need to always respect what they did for you, remember the good times, and cherish those memories.

REKINDLING A FORMER TERRIFIC RELATIONSHIP THAT ONCE TURNED SOUR

Sometimes people may not be terrific at a certain point in your life, but then become terrific again after they have gotten their own lives together and are happier. Sometimes people can stop being terrific because the pressures and circumstances in their own lives don't allow them to. Matt was on the verge of losing his business, his wife, and his home. With his investments going awry, his entire world was falling apart. He couldn't relate to anyone, and he retreated because he was so embarrassed. His best friend Steve couldn't understand why Matt would no longer take his calls and accept his invitations to play golf and tennis. Steve thought there must have been something that he did, but he couldn't figure out what. Upset, he went over to Matt's house to find out what was going on. Matt went ballistic and told Steve to never come over uninvited again.

Now Steve was convinced that it was something he either did or said that had turned Matt off to him. For nine months he racked his brain trying to figure out what he possibly could have done to upset Matt. One day he received a call from Matt, who opened up and told him that the reason he shunned him was because he was on the verge of financial ruin and felt embarrassed about his situation. Furthermore, he mentioned that he finally had lost it all and had to file bankruptcy. He didn't even have a job any longer. Relieved to know the real reason why Matt was so standoffish, Steve did all he could to help his once-terrific friend. Steve immediately got on the phone and made some calls. Matt had a job interview by the day's end and a new job by the week's end. Matt was deeply moved by Steve's dedication to their friendship, which also restored Matt's self-confidence. They began to spend more and more time together, and soon their terrific friendship was back on track. Steve reached out his hand in friendship, and even though it took Matt a while, he finally grabbed it, thereby revitalizing their relationship.

. . .

EVEN IF YOU haven't seen someone who was your most terrific friend in ages, or if you had a falling out at one point in time for whatever reason, your having respected that person's character makes it easier to reestablish ties if his or her character is still the same. When you do reestablish your relationship, there is a whole new set of rules and guidelines you both have to adhere to if you want the relationship to last.

Rules for Rekindling a Once-Terrific Relationship

1. Let go of past guilt and hard feelings.

2. Listen openly to the person's point of view, and objectively try to learn something from a past error you may have made in the relationship.

3. Don't get on the defensive.

4. Don't blame. Forget about whose fault it was. Start fresh.

5. Admit your mistakes readily and apologize openly, especially if you were at fault.

6. Don't hold back and edit; instead, say it all.

7. Never verbally attack or threaten the person.

8. Never hit below the belt in bringing things up about the past, or in discussing sensitive issues that could hurt the other person.

9. Don't use sarcasm or belittling humor.

10. Stick to the current issues. Never rehash what happened in the past.

11. Be conscious of your tone of voice. Don't use a cold, monotonous, or harsh tone. Instead, show enthusiasm and warmth.

Chapter 8

There Are Lots of Terrific People in the World!

- *A Terrific Child*
- *A Terrific Service Person*
- *A Terrific Health Professional*
- *Terrific Neighbors*
- *A Terrific Lover*
- *Terrific Parents*
- *Terrific Physically Challenged People*
- *Terrific Animals*

*T*hroughout this book, we have learned what traits constitute terrific people and how to surround ourselves with them in order to enhance every aspect of our lives. We have seen how to best attract other terrific people and how to become a terrific person to the person who matters the most—*you*. We have learned techniques that are designed to improve self-esteem and encourage growth. We have learned to treat ourselves with the love, kindness, and self-respect we so richly deserve, and not let anything or anyone reduce our self-worth. Finally, we have seen not only how to find, but how to keep and nurture those fantastic relationships with others. In dealing with terrific people and in being one yourself, you must continue to give in order to receive. You must continue to think of others just as much or even more than you think of yourself.

Perhaps the loveliest expression I have ever heard was "Every time someone does a good deed, an angel smiles in heaven." The people you will meet in the following paragraphs have definitely caused many angels to smile. Through their selfless deeds, these terrific people have gone far beyond the limits in touching the hearts and souls of others. Through their existence, they have definitely made this world a better place.

The stories that you are about to read may make you laugh, make you cry, intrigue you, and inspire you. Perhaps they will move you to become even more terrific than you already are. But, most of all, the stories will not only give you hope, but the reassurance that there are indeed terrific people in the world. You never again have to ask the question. "Are there any good people out there?" The answer is yes. Here are some of them:

A Terrific Child

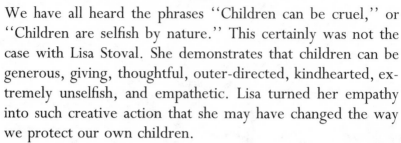

We have all heard the phrases "Children can be cruel," or "Children are selfish by nature." This certainly was not the case with Lisa Stoval. She demonstrates that children can be generous, giving, thoughtful, outer-directed, kindhearted, extremely unselfish, and empathetic. Lisa turned her empathy into such creative action that she may have changed the way we protect our own children.

Texas preteen Lisa Stoval was so distraught over the kidnapping of a young girl her age in a neighboring town that she vowed she would do all she could to help children who may be in danger. So she built a tiny hidden transmitter that could be used to track children miles away. Passionate in her quest, she researched her dream by writing to the Texas Parks and Wildlife Department about the tracking devices they used to locate wild animals.

Lisa further used her ingenuity to modify the device for use outside the body—as opposed to being implanted under the skin, as they are with animals. In addition, she was able to increase the tracking distance to a twenty-mile radius.

Lisa demonstrates that not only from "the mouths of babes" but from "the minds of babes" terrific things happen that can make the world a better and safer place to live. From the deepest sympathy of her sweet heart and tender soul came a brilliant thought put into action immediately, so that kidnapped and murdered "Amber" of Arlington, Texas didn't die in vain.

A Terrific Service Person

Norman Demers of Rhode Island has been a successful barber for over thirty years. He decided to give back some of his good fortune to others by giving free haircuts to senior citizens who were "shut-ins," too frail and ill to visit a barber. On his day off, Norman went to veterans hospitals, nursing homes, and housing projects where the elderly lived to wash, cut, and style their hair free of charge.

His good deeds touched not only the lives of those whose hair he cut, but the hearts of those who were close to them. The wife of one of his elderly patrons was moved to tears and was eternally grateful for Mr. Demers's efforts to make her husband more presentable and enhance his self-esteem during the last days of his life.

This unselfish barber took his only day off from work to give back to those who needed him found that his gesture was indeed far reaching.

A TERRIFIC HEALTH PROFESSIONAL

Dr. Jim Withers worked at a Pittsburgh hospital treating patients who could afford to see him. It disturbed him that there were people in his community who didn't have the means or the wherewithal to get treatment. So he filled his backpack with medicines and food and began treating homeless patients. Each day he wandered the streets looking for homeless people to help. Other doctors saw his unselfish devotion and kind and caring treatment of these people and offered to provide free treatment as well. The most rewarding experience for Dr. Withers was that his efforts helped eight of the homeless people he treated to get off the streets, back on track, and begin new lives. Today he and his team of doctors continue their efforts.

TERRIFIC NEIGHBORS

Fed up with panhandling, burglary, and vagrancy in his community, Brian Kito single-handedly began a private citizens' safety patrol to make his community safer for tourists, merchants, and elderly residents. Today he has over fifty volunteers. Thanks to Brian, Little Tokyo in downtown Los Angeles, California, has become the safe neighborhood it once was when he was growing up there.

A TERRIFIC LOVER

It is indeed a very terrific woman who would stay with a man for years, speaking to him daily, kissing and caressing him tenderly, and encouraging him with words of love and tenderness as he lies in a coma for four years. This is what Cecelia Orlandi of Modena, Italy, did when her boyfriend, Valerio Vasirani, was knocked unconscious after a car accident. Inevitably, her words of love and her constant affection had a great impact. Miraculously, Valerio woke up from his coma four years later. Even though his speech is still severely impaired, he is able to eat, drink, and to communicate with gestures. Cecelia continues to display her loyalty. She believes that one day the love of her life will speak to her, and that they will have a wonderful future, complete with marriage and children.

TERRIFIC PARENTS

When parents moan and groan because they don't have enough money to take care of their children, they need to look to Pat and Jill Williams of Orlando, Florida, for inspiration. People who have prejudiced or racist thoughts also need to meet the Williamses. These terrific people know firsthand that people are all alike under the skin. They know that everyone has the same needs: to be loved, accepted, and nurtured. They know this very well because they have adopted fourteen out of their eighteen children from such countries as Romania, Brazil, the Philippines, and Korea. Even a general manager's salary for the

Orlando Magic basketball team is stretched to the limit when there are twenty people to feed, clothe, and care for. However, this doesn't deter Pat and his wife. They have inner strength and tremendous spiritual faith that God has—and will continue to—provide them with the financial means to care for their huge multicultural family. Their tremendous love for their faith and for one another is so strong that it radiates across the world—shining on and embracing the lives of children who would otherwise never know about the power of love, much less what it is like to sleep in a clean bed, have enough food to eat, wear clothes that aren't filthy or full of holes, or go to a doctor whenever they get sick. Pat and Jill show us that love can conquer many obstacles.

TERRIFIC PHYSICALLY CHALLENGED PEOPLE

Anyone who feels sorry for a person who is physically challenged or who came from a dysfunctional family needs to take a good look at Jack Hutchings, whose alcoholic parents kicked him out of their home to fend for himself when he was sixteen years old. Jack Hutchings is blind. In order to survive, he got a job working for a small company that made tubing.

Although blind, Jack saw the future and realized that one day people would want the comfort of air conditioning in their cars. These cars would all require tubing in order to function. Not deterred by his blindness, he quit his job and independently started making the coiled tubing that the air-conditioning units would need in order to run properly. He sold them to manufacturers and soon his product became a huge success. Today Jack owns sixteen manufacturing plants nationwide, along with a waterfront home in Florida, a yacht, and two private jets.

When Jim Abbott, who was born without his right hand, was growing up in Michigan, nobody ever dreamed that he would bring so many people so much joy by becoming one of the top baseball players in the major leagues. The loving support of his family encouraged him to become a top quarterback in college and then become a member of the California Angels baseball team. At twenty-eight, this remarkable man has not only given others so much joy and inspiration, but he and his wife have supported many charitable causes to which he continues to give and give.

TERRIFIC ANIMALS

Ralph is a black Labrador retriever who is allowed to wander around his neighborhood freely. His owners never worry about him. Being exceptionally bright, he knows when to come home. He is the neighborhood mascot, and he is welcomed in other people's homes. The neighbors reassure his owners that he'll be safe. Every afternoon, when school lets out, he tags along with the young boys in the neighborhood.

One afternoon Ralph was visibly upset and grabbed one of the boys' pants legs. He began pulling the boy down the street. At first, all the boys thought it was a game. When they realized that Ralph kept barking and pulling the boy in the direction of the supermarket parking lot across the street, they all followed. Ralph jumped onto the hood of an old beat-up car and began to bark loudly. The four boys ran over to the car to see what was troubling Ralph—a crying baby was locked in the car with all the windows rolled up in the boiling heat. One of the boys got a rock and tried to break open the window while another boy got the manager of the supermarket, who called the police. They came quickly, broke into the car, and arrested the baby's father for child endangerment.

If it wasn't for Ralph, this baby might not be around today. Ralph was a hero. He got his photo in the paper and received an award for heroism, along with his four human friends, who also saved the child.

.   .   .

W E N E E D T O look up to these terrific individuals and hold them in the highest of esteem as they are truly our heroes— and the real stars.

We need to honor the real heroes—those people who care about others, who do whatever they can to unselfishly help their fellow man, and who attempt to lead their lives in a manner that inspires others, and does not repulse them.

As you have seen here, terrific people come in all different colors, shapes, sizes, ages, ethnic backgrounds, educational backgrounds—and even species. So the next time you have any doubt about the spirit of humanity, or are disappointed in people, reread this chapter. It is one of the best remedies for restoring your faith in others.

No matter how much technology surrounds us, we can never lose sight of the importance of human relationships.

So get out there right now and have a great time exploring all the different places and finding the terrific people who will introduce you to other terrific people, who will introduce you to other terrific people. After you have found them, make it a point to keep these terrific people in your life through nurturing, appreciating, and respecting them. It will bring you joy, lots of laughter, lots of smiles, lots of great feelings, lots of excitement, lots of new adventures, lots of hugs and kisses— and lots of love. It will bring you the life which you always dreamed of and which you are entitled to—guilt-free.

About the Author

DR. LILLIAN GLASS is known internationally as the "First Lady of Communication." When Dustin Hoffman needed to develop his "woman's voice" for *Tootsie,* when hearing impaired actress Marlee Matlin decided to speak publicly for the first time at the Academy Awards, when Sean Connery was worried about losing his distinctive voice following throat surgery, when Academy Award–winner Nicholas Cage needed to gain an accent for a movie role, and when international singing sensation Julio Iglesias needed to reduce his Spanish accent, they all turned to Lillian Glass.

Thousands of clients—famous, not-so-famous, and even infamous—have turned to Dr. Glass because they were eager to improve their communication skills and interactions with coworkers and loved ones.

With a strong academic background, M.S. from the University of Michigan, a Ph.D. from the University of Minnesota, and a postdoctorate degree from the UCLA School of Medicine, Dr. Glass has combined her skills in communication disorders, medical genetics, and social psychology to become one of the most renowned and well-respected communications specialists in the world.

She has touched and changed millions of people's lives not only through her private practices in Beverly Hills and Manhattan, but as a sought-after, highly entertaining, and charismatic motivational speaker. Her audiences have included corporate groups, legal organizations, and numerous professional associations across the United States and throughout the world.

Her best-selling books and tapes—which include *Talk to Win—6 Steps to a Successful Vocal Image, The World of Words—Vocabulary Training; Say It Right—How to Talk in Any Social or Business Situation; He Says, She Says—Closing the Communication Gap Between the Sexes;* and *Toxic People—10 Ways of Dealing with People Who Make Your Life Miserable*—are available worldwide.

Her no-nonsense, straightforward, yet sensitive and compassionate approach has made Dr. Lillian Glass one of the most sought-after media experts and personalities on television today. She also makes her message of "global peace through communication" known through radio and newspaper and magazine articles.

Index

Where to Get More Information for Dr. Glass's Products and Services

For more information send the following page in a
SELF ADDRESSED and STAMPED ENVELOPE TO:

Dr. Lillian Glass
C/O YOUR TOTAL IMAGE INC.
120 E. 87th St.
Suite P12F
New York, NY 10128

or PHONE (212) 946–5729   or FAX (212) 876–1642

Name _____

Address _____

City _____ State _____ Zip _____

Phone (   ) _____ Fax (   ) _____

OTHER BOOKS AND MATERIALS *by Dr. Glass* ____
  Lectures and Speaking Engagements ____
  Seminars in Your State ____
  Corporate Training Programs ____
  Audiotapes ____
  Videotapes ____
  Greeting Cards ____
  Individual Sessions ___ *(NYC) office* ___ *(LA) office* ___
    Phone _____
  Telephone, Audiotape, or Videotape Evaluation ____

If you enjoyed reading this book and would like to purchase the companion book, *Toxic People: 10 Ways of Dealing with People Who Make Your Life Miserable* (St. Martin's Press), you may order and purchase it at your local bookstore or feel free to call: 1-800-288-2131 to place an order.

LILLIAN GLASS Ph.D.
Author of
Attracting Terrific People

Toxic People

"Forget Dale Carnegie: Glass is riding to your rescue."
—*West Coast Review of Books*

10 ways of dealing

with people who make

your life miserable